The Chosen Journey

A Testimony of the High Calling of God

CAMILLE SPRINGER

CHAYIL WORKS
PUBLISHING

Copyright © 2025 Camille Springer

All rights reserved.

No part of this publication may be reproduced, distributed, or transmitted in any form or by any means, including photocopying, recording, or other electronic or mechanical methods, without the prior written permission of the publisher, except as permitted by Canadian copyright law. For permission requests, contact Chayil Works Publishing.

For privacy reasons, some names, locations, and dates may have been changed.

Book Cover designed by C. Springer

Unless otherwise noted, all scriptures are from the KING JAMES VERSION, public domain.

Scripture quotations marked (NLT) are taken from the Holy Bible, New Living Translation, copyright ©1996, 2004, 2015 by Tyndale House Foundation. Used by permission of Tyndale House Publishers, Carol Stream, Illinois 60188. All rights reserved.

Scripture quotations marked (HCSB) are taken from the HOLMAN CHRISTIAN STANDARD BIBLE, Copyright© 1999, 2000, 2002, 2003 by Holman Bible Publishers, Nashville Tennessee. All rights reserved.

Scripture quotations marked (AMP) are taken from the AMPLIFIED® BIBLE, Copyright© 1954, 1958, 1962, 1964, 1965, 1987 by the Lockman Foundation Used by Permission. (www.Lockman.org)

Published by Chayil Works Publishing.

www.chayilworkspublishing.com

ISBN:
978-1-0696418-0-9 (Print)
978-1-0696418-1-6 (eBook)

DEDICATION

This book is dedicated to the Chosen Ones – the black sheep, the rejected, the broken, the warriors, the seekers, and the dreamers. Without you, the Kingdom of God would be boring – so keep being you. You are loved and adored by God, and I hope you flourish in your uniqueness.

CONTENTS

	Acknowledgments	i
	Introduction	ii
1	The Foundations	Pg 1
2	The Encounter	Pg 16
3	The Tribulation	Pg 32
4	The Warfare	Pg 44
5	The Deliverance	Pg 64
6	The Calling	Pg 82
7	The Training	Pg 97
8	The Knowing	Pg 124
9	The Understanding	Pg 143
10	The Naming	Pg 154
11	The Promise	Pg 163
12	The Opposition	Pg 174
13	The Scourging	Pg 194
14	The Journey	Pg 209
15	Prayers for The Chosen	Pg 225
16	Questions for The Chosen	Pg 234

ACKNOWLEDGMENTS

Many thanks to my mother and father who raised me into the woman I am, who bore me up when I needed a shoulder to cry on, and who've always looked out for me. Also, thank you to my godparents, teachers, professors, spiritual leaders, encouragers, friends, and prayer partners who've transformed me into the well-rounded, skilled, and insightful human I've grown to be. Your contribution to my life as destiny helpers was exactly as God intended. And, greater than all these beautiful people, thank you to my Heavenly Father for enabling me to write and pour from a cup he's continued to fill.

INTRODUCTION

In the Western world, we've been taught to "logicize" everything. Meaning, we've been trained to believe that there is only a physical or materially observable reason for humankind's problems, experiences, histories, successes, and failures. Most people in the West worship the god of logic. They only trust what they can see and tangibly experience, otherwise they claim falsehood and imagination. People pride themselves on being able to logically and sensibly come to "reasonable" conclusions, no matter how erroneous or ridiculous they may be.

Then there are people like me. Although we too worshipped the god of logic, we had our worldview shifted by the God of Abraham, Isaac, and Jacob. We've been awakened, regenerated, and reformed and therefore, we view life and mankind through the spiritual knowledge introduced in the Holy Bible. People like me are who I like to call, **The Chosen Ones**.

It is through a relationship with God via Jesus Christ (in concert with the Holy Spirit) that we get to understand *true* spirituality and the *chosen journey* it invites us to take. The revelation in the Holy Bible peels back the layers on this divine journey and the phases involved.

A *Chosen One's* journey with God cannot be understood by human logic, however. And it's for this very reason that born again Christians appear odd to the world. Yahweh is a God that *"chooses the foolish things to confound the wise"* (1 Corinthians 1:27). He alone is the Divine Orchestrator for our perplexing, unique, and transformative stories. He simply will not share this glory with the god of logic, and that's why this journey cannot make sense through philosophical or formulative lenses.

For example, how does one go from depression, sexual immorality, anger, and confusion to being a Bible-thumping, Holy Spirit baptized, fire-talking, and holy-walking Christian? How does one transition from knowing little about scripture to actually living the written Word of God, and understanding spiritual revelation? Or how does one go from not knowing the real meaning of the Gospel of Jesus Christ to sharing that very Gospel with their fellowman? It's not a mystery (although it is); it's simply a journey – a heavenly-written story. It's my story, and it's one that I'll be sharing with you, the reader.

If you're still reading, I hope you know I had the audacity to write this book. A book that will give insight into a Christian's journey. A book that, God-willing, will give Jehovah the glory and honour he fully deserves. This book and its contents cannot be understood by a humanistic, worldly, or carnal mind. What is written here is purely spiritual, and these spiritual things can only be spiritually understood.

YHWH through the Ruach HaKodesh (Holy Spirit) has given me the assignment to share part of my story with you through this book. Woven into the fabric of these pages are biblical principles and my personal testimony, which can assist you in diving into a deeper relationship with God.

I hope you'll continue to read and allow God to walk you through this journey, showing you all the things He wants to reveal to your heart. My prayer is that after you finish reading this book that your life would be markedly transformed for the glory of Christ. Prayerfully consider everything written therein and be

INTRODUCTION

blessed. Let His Word dwell richly in you and keep an open mind.

Camille Springer
Author and Servant of Jesus Christ

"And I heard a loud voice saying in heaven, Now is come salvation, and strength, and the kingdom of our God, and the power of his Christ: for the accuser of our brethren is cast down, which accused them before our God day and night. And they overcame him by the blood of the Lamb, and by the word of their testimony; and they loved not their lives unto the death."

Revelation 12:10-11

The Chosen Journey

A Testimony of the High Calling of God

1 | THE FOUNDATIONS

"If the foundations be destroyed, what can the righteous do?"
Psalms 11:3

As with any journey, there is a beginning, a start, or a genesis. For both Christians and non-Christians, the beginning of their journey is initiated long before they are born or had any idea of their existence. This beginning we are speaking of is known as the *foundation*. The foundation is the spiritual cornerstone to every human's life.

According to the Merriam-Webster dictionary, one of the definitions of the word foundation is: "a basis (such as a tenet, principle, or axiom) upon which something stands or is supported." In construction, the foundation of our houses supports the building's entire structure. If the foundation is faulty, the house and everything in it could sink or collapse. Faulty foundations have led to catastrophic residential tragedies such as the 2016 Nanakaramguda collapse in Hyderabad, India, leaving 11 dead. However, many never consider that if the faulty foundations of physical buildings can cause so much turmoil, what about the faulty *spiritual foundations* of people?

A person's (spiritual) foundation is comprised of two main parts:
1. Their ancestral lineage or bloodline.
2. Their childhood and upbringing.

ANCESTRAL LINEAGE

Our forefathers always leave us a spiritual inheritance that is far more valuable than money, property, and insurance payouts. They set the tone for the quality of our lives. Often people say they love and would do anything for their children, grandchildren, and family members. Yet, they will not live righteous, holy, and set apart lives unto the Lord. They don't know that their loved ones can live pitiful, chaotic, and broken lives filled with suffering, resulting from sinful and wicked lifestyles.

> "Our ancestors sinned, but they have died— and we are suffering the punishment they deserved!" – **Lamentations 5:7 (NLT)**

> "You must not bow down to them or worship them, for I, the LORD your God, am a jealous God who will not tolerate your affection for any other gods. I lay the sins of the parents upon their children; the entire family is affected—even children in the third and fourth generations of those who reject me." – **Exodus 20:5 (NLT)**

Some members of the Church have sought to deny the existence of generational curses. They claim the only curse appointed unto men is the curse of sin that was brought through Adam & Eve's fall in the Garden of Eden. However, I have studied and found scripture after scripture that proves otherwise. God is an unchanging God, and his Word does not lie. Generational curses are a real *and* biblical thing! God has explicitly shown through his Word that if a person sins (intentionally, repeatedly, and unrepentantly), then he will curse that person *and* the coming generations of that individual's lineage.

> "The curse of the Lord is in the house **[household, family, descendants]** of the wicked: but he blesseth the habitation of the just." – **Proverbs 3:33** *[insert emphasis mine]*

> "I call heaven and earth to record this day against you, that I have set before you life and death, blessing and cursing: therefore choose life, that both thou and thy seed may live: That thou mayest love the Lord thy God, and that thou mayest obey his voice, and that thou mayest cleave unto him: for he is thy life, and the length of thy days: that thou mayest dwell in the land which the Lord sware unto thy fathers, to Abraham, to Isaac, and to Jacob, to give them." – **Deuteronomy 30:19-20**

A curse is the sanction of affliction, sickness, pain, suffering, tragedy, and/or disaster, due to breaking God's spiritual laws. Therefore, a curse needs a *reason* to exist. The reason for generational curses will always be the violation of God's statutes and commandments (found in the Bible), which are then perpetuated by each new generation. Think of generational curses as the negative cycles observed within a family generation after generation.

> "Behold, I set before you this day a blessing and a curse; A blessing, if ye obey the commandments of the Lord your God, which I command you this day: And a curse, if ye will not obey the commandments of the Lord your God, but turn aside out of the way which I command you this day, to go after other gods, which ye

have not known." – **Deuteronomy 11:26-28**

"If you don't listen, and if you don't take it to heart to honor My name," says Yahweh of Hosts, "I will send a curse among you, and I will curse your blessings. In fact, I have already begun to curse them because you are not taking it to heart. Look, I am going to rebuke your descendants, and I will spread animal waste over your faces, the waste from your festival sacrifices, and you will be taken away with it." – **Malachi 2:2-3 (HCSB)**

"Like a fluttering sparrow or a darting swallow, an undeserved curse will not land on its intended victim." – **Proverbs 26:2 (NLT)**

Just as God can curse those who descend from wicked forefathers, he can also bless the descendants of the righteous. It's important, especially if you have children or plan on having them, to live a righteous and holy life. If you don't, your sins can and will manifest as curses on your offspring. The curses and blessings God releases to people due to disobedience or obedience can be found in Deuteronomy 28 and Leviticus 26 (and other parts of the scriptures).

"And his mercy is on them that fear him from generation to generation." – **Luke 1:50**

"But showing faithful love to a thousand generations of those who love Me and keep My commands." – **Exodus 20:6 (HCSB)**

"And I will establish my covenant between me and thee and thy seed after thee in their generations for an everlasting covenant, to be a God unto thee, and to thy seed after thee." – **Genesis 17:7**

CHILDHOOD

Additionally, how a person is raised and the events of their childhood, have a profound effect on their life. This is why the Bible gives these instructions to parents:

> "Train up a child in the way he should go: and when he is old, he will not depart from it." – **Proverbs 22:6**

> "And, ye fathers, provoke not your children to wrath: but bring them up in the nurture and admonition of the Lord." – **Ephesians 6:4**

Children, when they are born, are innocent and new to the world. They have a purity that no adult can ever achieve because of this. But, as a child grows and is exposed to different things in life, their innocence dissolves.

Kids who are molested, abused, neglected, rejected, and mistreated by the adults in charge of them and their peers, often grow to be hardened men and women that display negative and life-altering behaviours. However, if a child is surrounded by love, care, attention, and kindness, that child often thrives and obtains different measures of success.

Childhood trauma can ruin our spiritual foundations, and this reality is becoming more evident in the observations of societal life. In fact, according to the Substance Abuse and Mental Health Services Administration, it is noted that, "More than two thirds of children reported at least 1 traumatic event by age 16." These traumatized children grow into the emotionally, mentally, and spiritually unstable adults we see today. For many, the words of Stewart Stafford couldn't be truer when he said, "Adulthood is an attempt to become the antithesis of the wounded child within us."

Unresolved childhood trauma and pain can lead to a life of tragedy. Many demons (familiar spirits) seek entrance into an individual's life in their younger years to engineer the destruction of their soul. Therefore, the childhood part of our foundation should and *must* be dealt with.

From a young age, a child's destiny can be determined by that child's behaviours, speech, interests, and mannerisms. The Bible reveals this fact in the Book of Proverbs:

> "Even children are known by the way they act, whether their conduct is pure, and whether it is right." – **Proverbs 20:11 (NLT)**

A young child should be exposed to the Word of God early at all costs. So many children have not had the experience of going to church or engaging in Bible study or Christian fellowship, and therefore, lack any understanding about God and his Word. Parents, grandparents, and elders are commanded in scripture to share about God, his ways, and his Word with the young upcoming generations. Sadly, many have removed this sacred duty from childrearing.

> "One generation shall praise thy works to another, and shall declare thy mighty acts." – **Psalm 145:4**

> "We will not hide them from their children, shewing to the generation to come the praises of the Lord, and his strength, and his wonderful works that he hath done. For he established a testimony in Jacob, and appointed a law in Israel, which he commanded our fathers, that they should make them known to their children: That the generation to come might know them, even the children

which should be born; who should arise and declare them to their children: That they might set their hope in God, and not forget the works of God, but keep his commandments: And might not be as their fathers, a stubborn and rebellious generation; a generation that set not their heart aright, and whose spirit was not stedfast with God. – **Psalm 78:4-8**

THE ROCK OF OUR FOUNDATION

Jesus Christ revealed something interesting during his ministry here on earth. He explained to his disciples how we can have the right foundation. The only correct spiritual foundation a man could ever have is in God and His Word, and this is what Yahweh was always trying to get Israel to understand. God is our rock and our firm foundation. When we make God the centre of our lives; when we become obedient to his Word and the leading of his Holy Spirit – we are building the right foundation on the Rock (Jesus Christ).

> "There is none holy as the Lord: for there is none beside thee: neither is there any rock like our God." – **1 Samuel 2:2**

> "And why call ye me, Lord, Lord, and do not the things which I say? Whosoever cometh to me, and heareth my sayings, and doeth them, I will shew you to whom he is like: He is like a man which built an house, and digged deep, and laid the foundation on a rock: and when the flood arose, the stream beat vehemently upon that house, and could not shake it: for it was founded upon a rock. But he that heareth, and doeth not, is like a man that without a foundation built an house upon the earth; against which the stream did beat vehemently, and immediately it fell; and the ruin of

that house was great." – **Luke 6:46-49**.

My Foundation

My mother was always very open with her own story as much as she was with the beginning of mine. You see, she married my father at 23 years old, and at 31 years old she was about to give birth to me. What she didn't know was that I was a covenant baby. Tragically, she had previously lost my brother to a miscarriage. And in the midst of that pain and loss, she prayed to God and asked him for a child. But God has a funny sense of humour. He rewards people's faith with great gifts, and truly that is what my mother saw me as – a gift.

Mum was raised by a strict but loving grandmother who made sure she knew of God and church. She recalled special holidays walking to church in newly made dresses and overly tight shoes, with a gladness and cheer at the simplicity of life at that time. Her grandmother made sure to speak love and prayer over her despite poverty and rejection, and this no doubt shaped my mother's destiny as well as my own.

But here she was. Over 30 and expecting the arrival of what she thought to be a baby boy. After she gave birth to me the doctor held me up and asked her, "Ma'am, what do you have here?"

"A boy," my mother answered.

The doctor asked Mum the same question again and she replied with the same answer. However, when the doctor shifted my umbilical cord out the way and asked my mother a third time, she responded with –

"A girl!"

And a girl I was. Born in 1996 on the little island of Barbados to two loving middle-class parents, who tried to give me as much of the world as possible. My childhood was very typical, and my parents loved watching me flourish. They were vigilant and caring, while correcting and disciplining me as they saw fit. However, the one thing they passed on to me from my early years was the importance of going to church. I was christened (dedicated to God) and raised in the Anglican church. My parents named me 'Camille Christina,' but I don't think they knew the spiritual implications of giving me those names (I'll talk about names later in this book).

Growing up, I listened to sermons, engaged in Sunday school, read Bible scripture when asked, and so on. At the time, I didn't realise how important this foundation would be as I matured later in life. What my parents gave to me was a good springboard for where I would be going in the future. Their contribution to my life based on the principle of acknowledging God, set me up for accomplishing my destiny.

Nevertheless, my mother made it clear to me that I was no ordinary child. I was always different from my peers. I spoke with authority, enjoyed spending lots of alone time in solitude; I was of a scientific mind while also being very artistic, and my diligence and focus set me apart from those the same age as me. I excelled academically and went to two of the best schools in my island. Later, I worked extremely hard to earn a Barbados Exhibition (a small scholarship) that helped me to travel abroad to study at the tertiary level.

I sang, played the guitar, and wrote poetry and music. Additionally, I loved history, anthropology, and doing research. My mother also noted my gift of discernment from a young age as well as my introversion. It was my curiosity as a child that actually brought me closer to knowing more about God, along with the spiritual events that took place on the journey.

But there were some stains in my childhood too. At the age of 8, I was exposed to pornography by stumbling on a collection of my uncle's adult content DVDs. In fact, my uncle was addicted to porn and never tried to hide this when I was a kid (his home was filled with it). This discovery led to me seeking and engaging with ungodly content (including masturbation). Even though my parents tried to protect me from such things, they were no match for the hidden influence of family. (**Side Note:** Parents reading this – be aware of the family members and friends you allow your children to be around. Many of these people have addictions, perversions, and spiritually unclean practices that could introduce your children to things they are not ready for, which can negatively influence them. Use discernment and be as watchful as possible.)

In addition, I was faced with rejection from my peers and low self-esteem from being an obese child. This further expanded to episodes of depression while I was a teenager. I somehow always felt misunderstood by the people around me – and I was right. I also never had any close long-lasting friendships – I was either too awkward or too disinterested/distant.

These circumstances in my childhood and adolescence led to me being a perfectionist and an overachiever. I figured my only way to let people see who I am was to be intelligent and excellent. When I was less than what I thought I should be, I would mentally and emotionally pummel myself. It was an endless cycle. But both my mother and father instilled good ethics, morals, and values that positively shaped my character. However, before I was even born, my foundation was already muddied.

My grandfather was a "lodge man" or Prince Hall Freemason. He left Barbados to serve in World War II and when he returned, he was said to have never been the same. My grandfather displayed signs of PTSD and had incidents of suicidal ideation and explosive outbursts of anger. He was also a philanderer and adulterer, who would frequently have extramarital affairs. These relationships resulted in children being born outside of his marriage, one of whom included my mother, who as I mentioned previously, was raised by my great-grandmother (my grandfather's mother).

Additionally, my mother's grandmother (on her mother's side) would at some point leave her young children in the care of a family friend to travel to Trinidad & Tobago (after many personal unfortunate instances, including finding her husband sleeping with another man). It was in this twin island-nation that my great-grandmother was exposed to and engaged in witchcraft. She returned to Barbados a different woman believing in various superstitions, rituals, and omens. She was initiated but was also said to be very religious.

It also didn't help that this same woman (my great-grandmother) had a curse placed upon her and her children by her own mother. After the disappointment and betrayal of not seeking her mother while on her deathbed, my great-great-grandmother said, "you and your children shall roam the earth like the seven seas." Well, "roam" they did. Everything about my great-grandmother and her children's lives was unstable and chaotic, which unfortunately was passed on to the next generation. As I learned later, these types of curses were very prominent in the family on my mother's side.

On my father's side, not much was told to me as a child. The lack of information on this side of my family was due to the family's divisive and dysfunctional dynamic. Most of my Dad's siblings would not speak to him, and he was only relatively close with two of his brothers. In essence, my father was the black sheep of the family.

Nonetheless, I was raised around my Dad's mother and was only told tidbits about my ancestry from her. Yet, I noticed a curious trait among my uncles, aunts, and cousins from that side of the family. Nearly all of them had an issue with sexual sin or perversion. Either they were homosexual, committed adultery, consumed pornography, had children out of wedlock, or were womanizers. Very few of them actually got married and had long-lasting, happy marriages. Even my grandmother had her first few children out of wedlock before being married. Out of all of my father's siblings, my Dad had the longest and most stable marriage.

On both sides of my parents' families, there were also trends of illnesses such as diabetes, heart disease, cancer, and high blood pressure. Everyone was either sick or managing some kind of chronic non-communicable disease.

It wasn't until I got into a relationship with Jesus Christ that the Holy Spirit started to reveal what was hidden in my childhood and ancestry. Even as a child I would be inquisitive and ask questions about God, religion, and purpose. I was searching for answers and never got them until later in my early adulthood. My foundation led me down a road to encounter the God of the universe.

2 | THE ENCOUNTER

"And it shall come to pass afterward, that I will pour out my spirit upon all flesh; and your sons and your daughters shall prophesy, your old men shall dream dreams, your young men shall see visions."
Joel 2:28

Powerful callings are uncovered and released via powerful encounters with God. This isn't conjecture. It's simply a scriptural fact. Every born-again Christian man, woman, and child had an encounter with God before embracing salvation. Some people's encounter may have been simple, textbook, and easy. Others experienced an encounter that knocked them off their feet and propelled them into uncharted territories in the Kingdom of God.

Moses encountered the I AM through the burning bush and was released as a governmental prophet and deliverer to the nation of Israel in Egypt. The encounter Moses had with God would go on to bear fruit in that multiple nations' destinies were established based on the acceptance of his calling and execution of leadership.

"Now Moses kept the flock of Jethro his father in law, the priest of Midian: and he led the flock to the backside of the desert, and came to the mountain of God, even to Horeb. And the angel of the Lord appeared unto him in a flame of fire out of the midst of a bush: and he looked, and, behold, the bush burned with fire, and the bush was not consumed. And Moses said, I will now turn aside, and see this great sight, why the bush is not burnt. And when the Lord saw that he turned aside to see, God called unto him out of the midst of the bush, and said, Moses, Moses. And he said, Here am I. And he said, Draw not nigh hither: put off thy shoes from off thy feet, for the place whereon thou standest is holy ground. Moreover he said, I am the God of thy father, the God of Abraham, the God of Isaac, and the God of Jacob. And Moses hid his face; for he was afraid to look upon God." – **Exodus 3:1-6**

Again, Apostle Paul encountered Jesus Christ as Saul of Tarsus on the road to Damascus. This encounter along with some discipleship from Ananais, catapulted Paul into his destiny as one of the most influential apostles of the early church. We still quote scriptures written by his hand to this very day, learning how to conduct ourselves as Believers in Christ Jesus.

"And Saul, yet breathing out threatenings and slaughter against the disciples of the Lord, went unto the high priest, And desired of him letters to Damascus to the synagogues, that if he found any of this way, whether they were men or women, he might bring them bound unto Jerusalem. And as he journeyed, he came near Damascus: and suddenly there shined round about him a light from heaven: And he fell to the earth, and heard a voice saying unto him, Saul, Saul, why persecutest thou me? And he said, Who art thou, Lord? And the Lord said, I am Jesus whom thou persecutest: it is hard for thee to kick against the pricks. And he trembling and astonished said, Lord, what wilt thou have me to do? And the Lord said unto him, Arise, and go into the city, and it shall be told thee what thou must do." – **Acts 9:1-6**

With these two examples in mind, we can see that ordinary people can be called by God through unusual, supernatural experiences and then used extraordinarily for God's glory. People encounter God in churches, apartments, cars, supermarkets, showers – anywhere. It is the encounter that causes us to believe in Jesus. It's the encounter that makes us fully convinced of his presence, love, and plan for us. The encounter obliterates doubt, uncertainty, and reveals the God of Heaven to lowly man. We experience healing, joy, awe, reverence, and pure love in the encounter. Jesus in this very hour is seeking to reveal himself to men in the realm of encounter.

However, sometimes we limit our understanding of how God can draw men to encounter him. When I reviewed the scriptures, I came to understand that one of the most potent and frequent ways God introduced himself to people was through dreams. In the Bible, people from all walks of life encountered God in the night watches and seasons, and through these encounters, they formed covenants with Yahweh, and received callings, blessings, impartations, instructions, and wisdoms from God.

Take Joseph for example. Being the youngest and most favoured son of Jacob (Israel), he received the call to government, authority, and leadership through God distilling revelation to him in his dreams. Joseph was encountering God through these prophetic dreams and receiving a snapshot of the future God had for him and his family.

"And Joseph dreamed a dream, and he told it his brethren: and they hated him yet the more. And he said unto them, Hear, I pray you, this dream which I have dreamed: For, behold, we were binding sheaves in the field, and, lo, my sheaf arose, and also stood upright; and, behold, your sheaves stood round about, and made obeisance to my sheaf. And his brethren said to him, Shalt thou indeed reign over us? or shalt thou indeed have dominion over us? And they hated him yet the more for his dreams, and for his words." – **Genesis 37:5-8**

But even before Joseph, Jacob himself experienced a heavenly encounter with God as he fled from the fury of his brother Esau, which can be found in Genesis 28:10-17. In Jacob's dream encounter, he saw the angels of God ascending and descending on a stairway/ladder that reached all the way into heaven, indicating the location he was in was a portal or gateway to the heavenlies. God spoke to Jacob in the dream and gave him a covenant promise that included the generations to come. Because of this, he named the place he was in Bethel (meaning house of God).

King Solomon, despite being raised in the affluence of the royal house of David, was never recorded in the Bible having a serious encounter with God until he took the throne after his father. God, being pleased with Solomon's virtue and sacrifice, met with Solomon in the dream realm twice. These meetings with God in dreams allowed Solomon to receive unusual and supernatural wisdom, with the Bible noting him as the wisest man that ever lived. See 1 Kings 3:5,9-10 and 2 Chronicles 7:11-12.

Encounters with God through dreams are where Our Heavenly Father invites our spirit man to commune with him while our bodies slumber. We are a tri-part being (body, soul, spirit) according to scripture [1 Thess. 5:23], even as Jehovah is a triune God (Father, Son, Holy Spirit) [Matt. 28:19]. Though our physical bodies seek rest, our human spirits never have need of it, and therefore, are still active while we sleep.

> "For God speaketh once, yea twice, yet man perceiveth it not. In a dream, in a vision of the night, when deep sleep falleth upon men, in slumberings upon the bed; Then he openeth the ears of men, and sealeth their instruction, That he may withdraw man from his purpose, and hide pride from man. He keepeth back his soul from the pit, and his life from perishing by the sword." – **Job 33:14-18**

My primary life-changing encounter with God was through the ministry of dreams. Some of my most powerful revelations and understandings came when the Lord spoke to me in dreams. Prophecies, wisdoms, and impartations were released to me from the God of Heaven through dreams.

God is revealing Himself to people all over the world at night while they sleep. Unfortunately, most people brush-off their dreams and believe they have no real meaning. Medical and psychiatric professionals have 'psychologized' revelatory streams, assuming hallucinations, stress, and mental disorders as the root of men receiving downloads from the spiritual realm. This couldn't be further from the truth. Christians should pay attention to their dreams! It is vitally important to know how and what God is trying to communicate with you.

Throughout the rest of this book, I will be referring to some of the dreams I've received to illustrate certain points. If you are receiving dreams and don't know what they mean, there are four things you need to do:

1. Strengthen your relationship with God via Holy Spirit. This step may involve you going into a period of consecration, prayer, Bible study, and even fasting.
2. Write down or record the dreams you are receiving. I recommend getting a journal specifically for your dreams and visions, and the prayers associated with them.
3. Start asking God about your dreams in prayer. Ask him what the symbols, phrases, colours, objects, numbers, animals, and scenes mean. He will answer you (Jeremiah 33:3).
4. Purchase Biblical dream/vision dictionaries and reference books by Christian authors who have the gift of interpretation of dreams. I *highly* recommend books on this subject by Dr. Joe Ibojie.

My Encounter

My own encounter with God came at an odd space in my life. It should be noted here that I had various experiences with God in my childhood, but none that transformed my life so acutely as the one I had while in university.

As a child and teenager during my depressive episodes, I would feel the tangible presence of God around me. I would also experience the conviction of the Lord concerning negative behaviours and attitudes I would express. I remember talking to God while laying on my bed preparing to go to sleep as a pre-teen and sensing him talking back to me. I also remember having vivid and extensive dreams that I couldn't fully understand. During rough times in my life as a teen, I would be sensitive to the fact that I would see the manifestation of demonic spirits around me, and I would also hear them attempting to speak to me. Experiencing these incidents of demonic presence would draw me closer to God. Often, I never told my parents that I was seeing or hearing these spiritual things. All of these were experiences leading up to the big encounter.

When I left Barbados to pursue my undergraduate degree, I had no idea that God was running after me. I had read about God, sang about him, and heard people talk about him, but I really didn't *know* him. However, I was religious and brought my mother's KJV bible and my own NIV bible with me to Canada on my academic journey. This turned out to be one of the best decisions I ever made.

Between the second to third year of my program, I grew an unusual hunger for the Word of God. I remember picking up the

KJV bible and would read chapter after chapter for hours into the early morning. At the time, I made friends with someone who also had a Christian upbringing, and that's how I started attending a small Pentecostal church in my university's town. What was interesting was that whatever section of the Bible I was studying at the time; the pastor would preach about it on the Sundays that I attended. It was like a *'God wink,'* and leaving service gave me a better understanding of what I was reading in the Good Book.

Now here's where things get intriguing. I was changing and didn't even realise it. The Word of God was literally transforming me from the inside out. I had stopped entertaining pornographic material, watching certain TV shows, and was seriously searching for the truth of God. I used to listen to a man of God, Kevin LA Ewing, teach and preach on YouTube, which helped me understand my dreams and prayer better. And I even started talking with a former school mate of mine who seemed versed in the scriptures, and we would have all types of discussions on Bible history, theology – and even Hebrew Israelitism.

All of this went on for months, until one night when I was in my bedroom playing music and relaxing. Suddenly, I heard a voice say, *"You need to stop listening to this music!"* The voice was urgent, insistent, and very authoritative. But…I was obedient. I rose from my bed, went to my laptop, and started deleting all the mainstream/secular music I had downloaded. I even started to delete songs from my iPod. This was an odd experience, and I had no idea why I was even doing what I was doing. All I became aware of was that the music I was used to listening to was filled with perversion, witchcraft, anger, murder, fear, and uncleanness. Therefore, I needed to remove this type of music from my life. It was tough to give up the music that I liked, but I became more aware of this type of music's effect on me, and I just obeyed.

Looking back, this was my first real exposure to hearing God speak to me. And he wasn't done yet revealing his voice to me. In the first week of December 2017 during my semester exams, I had a dream:

My mother and I were walking together in the part of Barbados where she grew up. For some reason, we walked up to a house in the neighbourhood (I wasn't sure who lived there in the dream). Somehow in the dream I had x-ray vision, and I could see an evil tan coloured dog inside the house. Suddenly, this dog came out of the house and pounced to attack my mother and I. Strangely, a huge rock appeared in my right hand, and I aimed and threw the rock at the dog. To my surprise, the force of the impact caused flesh to rip away from the dog's mouth, exposing his teeth, and injuring him. Through the x-ray vision I seemed to have in this dream, I saw the dog run quickly and scared into a trap door inside the house.

I woke up from the dream. But the same urgent, insistent, and authoritative voice said, *"Write this dream down!"* It's then that I decided to start keeping a journal for my dreams and prayers. I just knew immediately from the dream that I had a spiritual victory against evil forces combating against me. The rock in my hand that I used to injure the malevolent dog, represented my prayers that would serve to protect me and my family (my mother represented my family in the dream). The Lord would later let me know that my salvation, discernment, and intercession, would be crucial in influencing the salvation and enlightenment of my family.

Afterwards, I started to have dreams of the Bible open before me, and I would hear a voice uttering scripture over me. I would wake up always trying to remember the specific book the Bible was open to and the scripture that was spoken. I also had other dreams during this time, but the Lord will not permit me to share them in this book.

Now, at this point you may have thought that you've read the encounter. But what I know now is that all of these events during this period were just seasonings to the *big* encounter. The major encounter happened when my parents were visiting me that same year for Christmas. They flew in to spend some quality time with me. But even *they* noticed something about me had changed. My mother constantly commented on what appeared to be my new "religious flare," because I had convictions about not celebrating certain holidays anymore. Needless to say, what my parents had envisioned for a nice holiday with their daughter turned out to be anything but.

Yet, God was moving. On December 27th, 2017, I was alone in my bedroom while my parents slept in another room. I was pensive but felt something tugging at me. I had read a prayer on a man of God's website, and decided to write it down, but instead of keeping the prayer as is, I filled the prayer up with the scriptures I had been learning and laying out what was in my heart to God. In the prayer, I was repenting for sin, asking God to manifest himself in my life, and asking him to deliver me from things that seemed to plague me. I laid bare all my faults and insecurities to the Father.

While writing it out in my journal, I felt the heavy presence of God and my entire body felt like it was on fire (like if I was completely covered in hot charged electricity). As I finished writing, I turned my head and saw a menacing demonic entity sink into my bed. Before it vanished, I saw that this demon looked as if it had the head of a human and jellyfish merged together and was very translucent. Weird, right? However, this occurrence didn't phase me. With reverence, I decided to say the prayer I wrote out loud. When I uttered those words verbally something changed drastically. The spirit realm was stirring and responding to what I did and said, and the fire I was clothed in only seemed to get hotter. The power of the tongue was at work and shifted the atmosphere. But even after this clearly supernatural thing occurred…I decided to go to sleep.

In retrospect, I was experiencing an Acts chapter 2 moment. I was bathed in fire because I was being baptized with the Holy Spirit's *fire*, just like how John the Baptist prophesied thousands of years before. The demonic entity I saw was afraid of that fire – that's why it disappeared before me.

> "I indeed baptize you with water unto repentance. but he that cometh after me is mightier than I, whose shoes I am not worthy to bear: he shall baptize you with the Holy Ghost, and with fire." – **Matthew 3:11**

> "And when the day of Pentecost was fully come, they were all with one accord in one place. And suddenly there came a sound from heaven as of a rushing mighty wind, and it filled all the house where they were sitting. And there appeared unto them cloven tongues like as of fire, and it sat upon each of them." – **Acts 2:1-3**

Sleep is vital to the human body, but dreams are a vital part of the spiritual language God uses to communicate with me. At the time, I didn't fully grasp this concept. But the night I fell asleep after praying my prayer, I understood it fully. I understood Yahweh was the God who answers by fire, and the God of visions and dreams. I clearly understood that Satan was the engineer of destruction, and that God exposes the plans of the enemy via dreams and visions.

Also, the understanding the Lord gave me is that *not all* dreams come from God – the enemy plants evil dreams into our dreamscape to pollute our destinies and deposit demonic poison in our lives. The enemy also sends dreams to deceive us away from the path God has for us, and so we have to carefully assess the dreams and visions we receive. That night I had 3 dreams, back-to-back.

Dream #1:
I was in what appeared to be an old Italian Mafia-styled living room. There were leather couches, and a silver platter with a bottle of brandy and glasses on a table. People that I didn't know were standing around having conversations with each other. Suddenly, a dark figure appeared before me, dressed in a black cloak like the grim reaper. I knew it was a man, but I couldn't see his face, and his head was covered with the cloak's hood. I discerned in the dream that this was a warlock. Out of nowhere, he held out a black box in front of him and then proceeded to open this box in my direction. A HUGE yellow and green scaled snake jumped out of the box and sprang in my direction to attack me. I found my self running away around the room to escape the snake's attacks, but every direction I went the snake darted

that way too. The people in the living room just stood looking at what was happening to me, but no one came to my aid. I kept trying to dodge the snake's fierce onslaught, and the dream ended with the snake pouncing to bite me.

I woke up from this dream shaken up, but I immediately started to pray and cancelled the effects of the dream. This dream was from the kingdom of darkness. Satan and his cohorts were upset at what God was doing in my life, and that warlock was sent to release that demonic serpent to destroy me. It was a vicious attack. I then went back to sleep.

Dream #2:
I saw myself walking around the city where my university was located. Suddenly, I heard a voice echoing, "RELEASE ME, RELEASE ME!" As I heard this voice, I also heard chains rattling and the dream shifted to where I saw what appeared to be a prison cell. In the dream, I felt something stirring within me.

I woke up to audibly hearing the same voice I heard in my dream saying, "Release me, release me!" But to my shock, I felt something *physically leave* my body. It was an experience I still have trouble explaining. I felt something other than me, another entity, break free from my human body…on my bed in my own bedroom! The best description is that when I jolted awake, I felt an invisible being detach and come out of my abdominal and chest area, and I released it with a big "humph!" I knew right away that some form of deliverance just took place, starting in the dream realm. Again, I prayed about the dream and what happened, and then I went back to sleep.

Dream #3:
I was in a plain and saw before me a brass statue, with the top of it having the shape of a Buddha head. Instantly, I saw this brass statue unexpectedly explode in front of me with shards of brass flying in my direction.

I woke up with the feeling of the shards of the statue in my dream clinging to my face. I had never worshipped Buddha in my life or followed the tenets of Buddhism. But in this dream, I believe Buddha represented a major idol being destroyed in my life – since I was now only following the path Yahweh had for me and leaving everything else behind. I prayed about this dream even as I prayed about the previous two.

Something spiritually happened. An echo, a deliverance, a confirmation, an imprint, an explosion. It seemed evident to me that God responded to my prayer that night, and the dark forces that be did *not* like it.

I didn't tell my parents what I experienced that night. Instead, I tried to do activities with them before their return flight. But in the short while between them leaving and that fateful December night, what I recognized to be God's voice got stronger. I was prompted and convicted about unforgiveness by that voice. I was told to apologize to people I had offended by that voice. And stranger still, I obediently did everything I was told to do.

How could I tell someone about what I experienced without them thinking I was crazy? You, reading what I just wrote in this book probably think I'm crazy.

One thing's for sure, at the time that all of this was happening:

1. I was hearing God's voice and His instructions.

2. I turned away and repented of sin.
3. I was being educated about the revelatory realms, particularly, of dreams/visions.
4. I experienced a spiritual regeneration and transformation.
5. I knew that evil spiritual forces were targeting me.
6. I had an intense love and hunger for the Word of God.

What I didn't know going into 2018, is that what I experienced was just the beginning. All hell was about to break loose in a fierce tribulation.

3 | THE TRIBULATION

> "Although affliction cometh not forth of the dust, neither doth trouble spring out of the ground; Yet man is born unto trouble, as the sparks fly upward."
> **Job 5:6-7**

There is one thing that is common to all people besides death. No matter how wealthy, poor, successful, or unsuccessful a person is, they have all experienced pain and suffering. Now, the pain and suffering they've experienced may not be the same situationally or contextually – but it's still very much valid. I've found this to be more and more true as I navigate life.

An affluent person does not know the pain and suffering of the homeless and destitute. But the impoverished know nothing of the sufferings of betrayal and jealousy that the wealthy often experience. Everyone you meet can tell you tales of the seasons of pain and suffering they've had to endure. You'll hardly find an accomplished person who hasn't endured some sort of pain and suffering.

There's a verse in the Bible that I've learned to enjoy. This verse softens your heart, and makes you look at life in general with a sobering and grateful perspective.

Job 14:1:

"Thus is the man born of woman, and he is few of days and suffers terror." **(ABPE)**

"Man born of a woman, living for a short time, is filled with many miseries." **(DRB)**

"Man, who is born of a woman, is of few days, and full of trouble." **(NHEB)**

We're all here born from the womb of our mothers and we all go through some type of trouble, terror, misery, suffering, pain, trial, or tribulation. When we understand this principle, we see people differently because it humanizes them. We're then able to respond to those around us with love, empathy, and consideration. Because life is short, and everybody is going through or has gone through something adverse.

Some of the "trouble" spoken about in Job 14:1 includes tribulation. By definition, tribulation means 'a state of great trouble or suffering.' It's interesting to me that the Bible mentions so much about tribulation, pain, and suffering, yet it's not taught very often in modern churches. Personally, I believe many church leaders have done a disservice by not teaching why tribulations exist, and how God uses them not only to transform His people, but for Him to get glory.

"Rejoicing in hope; patient in tribulation; continuing instant in prayer." – **Romans 12:12**

> "And not only so, but we glory in tribulations also: knowing that tribulation worketh patience." – **Romans 5:3**

There are people all over the world asking the question, "Why does God allow suffering?" They view the sufferings of life as a discredit to God, his goodness, and his divine plan. When they ask the above question, they either have an accusatory or confused tone. People are just completely unaware that much of the suffering we experience is due to the sins of mankind and the fallen nature of the world. They also are not humble or mature enough to know that suffering can in some ways be good. In fact, the psalmist wrote, "My suffering was good for me, for it taught me to pay attention to your decrees." (Psalm 119:71 [NLT]).

If life was peachy all the time, many of us would rise up in pride and refuse to seek or acknowledge God. It took me enduring my own sufferings (which I'll be discussing shortly), to understand that God uses our sufferings to draw us closer to him. When we become closer to God by enduring suffering it allows him to impart his will and guide us in truth. It causes us to be more aware of our Heavenly Father and we start to bear spiritual fruit. Therefore, the Christian perspective of tribulation and suffering is very different from that of the world.

Tribulation, pain, and suffering:

- Produce Godly character in us (process of sanctification).
- Strengthen us in areas where we are weak.
- Allow us to share in the sufferings of our Lord and Saviour Jesus Christ.
- Tests us in areas where God is trying to transform us.

- Prepares us for spiritual and physical promotion/elevation.
- Draws us to prayer, fasting, and consecration.
- Are used as tools for correction or chastening by God (when we step outside of his will or disobey Him).

My Tribulation

I was in a massive dining hall with a very long table having a purple tablecloth and decorated with finery. Decadent food was laid out to meet every indulgence and delight, ready for those seated around the table to partake of. I was seated at the table and there was a woman I did not recognise seated beside me. There were others seated around the table, and they were the picture of enjoyment, laughter, and happiness. This was a feast in a room full of splendour and joy. We were in a mansion and that's why the dining hall was so big. Suddenly, everyone rose from the table and headed toward another section of the mansion. For some reason I followed the woman who was seated beside me (we seemed to get along) and she came to the bottom of a massive golden staircase. She turned back to me with a smile on her face and said, "Welcome to the family of God," and we headed toward the ascent.

Shortly after my parents returned to Barbados from their visit with me in Canada, I had the above dream. I woke up from it wondering what it meant. As I've grown with Father, I came to understand that it was an introduction or initiation into the Kingdom of God. Everything about the dream was flavoured with royalty and sweetness. However, I wondered why I couldn't experience the same joy and harmony in my waking life.

As I pointed out in chapter 2, all hell broke loose after my encounter with God in December 2017. The unseen realm became realer to me than ever as I started to experience a myriad of spiritual attacks (I'll discuss this warfare in the next chapter). I was depleted and, in some ways, even defeated.

I remember going to the little Pentecostal church in my university's town, and each Sunday I would cry my heart out. I knew I looked haggard, disheveled, and broken, only because I saw faint concern in the faces of those around me in the church leadership and congregation. I tried to talk to the pastor about some of what I was experiencing (see chapter 4) but was met with an apathetic and dismissive attitude. You see, I tried to explain to him that I was being demonically attacked, but he didn't believe Christians could have demons or be demonically oppressed. So, every Sunday I wept where I sat in the church, totally confused, pained, and hurting, wondering why no body understood. Could they not see or discern what was happening to me? Why was no one talking to me about deliverance? Was I the only person experiencing this?

In addition, I was being urged by the Holy Spirit to get water baptised. The problem with that stemmed from the lack of understanding from the pastor. I didn't trust him and therefore, didn't know how to go about being baptised. I also didn't know how to go about seeking baptism at another church. God's urgency in the matter even caused me to attempt to baptise myself in my apartment bathtub. I was supremely frustrated in this season of my life. I was looking to the church I attended for answers, but I found none.

Instead, I found churches and preachers online on YouTube and Facebook and listened to them. Now that I've matured, I know that every preacher ministering online is not reliable or credible. However, the Holy Spirit was drawing me to certain ministries and as I listened to the preaching and teaching, it directly ministered to me, my situation, and the things to come. I took notes, looked up the scriptures, studied the contexts all on my own.

During this time, God also led me to buy books written by authors and ministers such as Derek Prince, Apostle John Eckhardt, Rev. James Solomon, and others. I was also led to buy a Bible dictionary and study materials. Outside of completing my class assignments, I spent hours studying the Bible and reading several Christian books.

The spiritual diet that I developed got the attention of my parents. They noted that I would talk with them about certain things and was able to recite Bible verses word for word. Considering my parents never enforced Bible study in the home growing up, this newfound ability to know the Bible like I did caught them off-guard. But with each passing day my parents grew more and more worried about me. Honestly, I was worried about me. My mom being the way she was, started to have conversations with some work friends who were more spiritually in-tune than her. Without even meeting face-to-face, just based on her description of me and what I was going through, my mother's colleagues told her that I was anointed and had a calling on my life. When she told me about it, I thought, "what's all of this about?" I had no clue. "Why would God call me? I'm just a nobody," I said.

I was completely struggling. None of my roommates, workmates, peers, or family members knew of the terrors I was experiencing each day. I hid the information about my struggle from them, but the struggle painfully showed in every area of my life. I have no idea how I managed to still graduate university with honours. I could hardly sleep, I was not eating, I wasn't keeping up with my hygiene, and I was always constantly crying and depressed.

I didn't have the peace or joy that God provides as I had read it in the Word. I was also very much broke at the time. Not because I wasn't working, but because I was giving so much of my earnings to the less fortunate and needy in my area. Every time I was in the inner city, there was always a homeless person I would either give money or food to.

Yet, all around me was chaos, pain, and trauma. It was only compounded by the fact that it seemed *no one* understood. They only saw the outward downward spiral but didn't know why. Folks concluded that I was going through a mental breakdown, but I knew that was not the case. There was a reason behind what was taking place, and I was still sane enough to get good grades and engage in some social activities. The reason was not psychological, but very much spiritual.

By God's divine grace, I met an evangelistic pastor who newly took up Bible studies at the little Pentecostal church I attended. For the purposes of protecting his identity, I'll call him Pastor A. He was a very compassionate and kind man, and as I got to know him, I learned that he evangelised and did ministry in countries like Uganda and Greece. Pastor A was passionate about the Word of God, and I guess he saw something in me that I didn't even see in myself. I engaged in the Bible studies and prayer sessions, and he saw my hunger for the Word and desire for the things of God. I believe Pastor A perceived something was off kilt in my life, but he didn't fully understand it. We built up a nice rapport, and he was simply glad that a university student was taking the time to pursue and be on fire for God.

But something happened. After over a year of this ongoing spiritual crisis and worrying my parents to death, the Holy Spirit urgently woke me up in April of 2019.

"Camille, you need to call Pastor A and let him know that something is wrong. He will help you," said Holy Spirit.

Although I heard the voice of the Holy Spirit clearly telling me what I should do, I still decided to get up to go to work. Well, as you can imagine, it didn't go well. While attending to my duties, I was so tormented I completely burst into tears and broke down in the office. All of my coworkers and supervisors thought I was simply a university student in a severe mental health crisis, and they asked me if I wanted them to book an appointment with campus counselling services. I politely declined, but I did ask to leave my shift, and they agreed.

While in the campus parking lot, I did what Holy Spirit told me to do earlier in the morning. I called Pastor A and told him something was wrong, and that God told me to contact him. I could hear the concern and care oozing through the phone from his voice. He said he would get dressed and come pick me up. Within half an hour I was getting into his car. I had tears streaming down my face, I stunk, and looked horrible. Pastor A drove me to my apartment to collect a few belongings and then afterward drove to he and his wife's house. This lovely retired Christian couple opened their home to me, gave me a room, cooked for me, and started discipling me even further.

Due to all the chaos, I couldn't focus and had to defer the last exam of my final semester. Pastor A and his wife took me to a doctor who prescribed anxiety medication and provided me with a note for the deferral. I had no idea I would end up spending five long weeks under their roof. Five long weeks still tormented. Five long weeks still away from family. Five long weeks still in bondage. Pastor A and his wife didn't understand what I was telling them and told me that I was confused and in error. They didn't believe that I had generational curses, or demons, or needed deliverance and inner healing. I was told to stop worrying about those things, to trust God, and prepare for my deferred exam and pending graduation.

I was crushed. I wanted to know why they didn't understand. They prayed in tongues, they had encounters with Holy Spirit, they preached and ministered internationally. How could they not believe what I was telling them; what Holy Spirit was telling me? In this season, I gained an important understanding: not all Christians are able to receive certain revelations. God showed me in that season that spiritual blindness and religion were at work in this beloved couple – that's why they didn't understand.

Pastor A told me he studied at seminary, and that what I was telling him was incorrect. I obviously didn't agree with him because what I was experiencing and reading in the scriptures implied otherwise. Yet, God used Pastor A and his wife in this period of my tribulation to help me gain some strength through their prayers and encouragement. To this day I am thankful to them and what they imparted to me during this rough time.

Just before I left to go back to Barbados at my parents' insistence, I was crying in the little room I had in Pastor A's house.

It was then that I heard Holy Spirit say, *"Camille, [your] training starts now. It's time for you to be used. But first we have to deal with your foundation."*

God had reassured me that the deliverance I was seeking for so long; I would finally get it when I left my university's little town. I didn't know what came next, but I knew I needed to trust God more than ever. He carried me on that airplane back to my island, and he surely had something planned.

4 | THE WARFARE

"For we wrestle not against flesh and blood, but against principalities, against powers, against the rulers of the darkness of this world, against spiritual wickedness in high places."
Ephesians 6:12

All around us is a realm that is unseen. New Agers and spiritualists will refer to this unseen realm as the 4th or 5th dimension, which they can 'ascend' to and attain some sort of 'godhood'. As much as the anatomical design of our physical eyes allows us to view and interpret the world around us, we need our spiritual eyes to see what lies beyond the veil. Physicists see the world through formulas, theories, and dark/light matter. But there is something that scientists can never fully grasp or explain – *the supernatural* – which is why they've created a philosophical area of study called *metaphysics*.

The most basic truth every Christian should know, is that: we are spiritual beings having a physical existence and experience on earth. Everything that manifests or exists in the earth first had to exist in the spiritual unseen realm. Nothing happens on planet earth without spiritual influence or clearance. This is the true reality of how God constructed the universe to operate. It's a reality most scientists will never accept because it would also mean acknowledging a Divine Creator.

> "For through him God created everything in the heavenly realms and on earth. He made the things we can see and the things we can't see— such as thrones, kingdoms, rulers, and authorities in the unseen world. Everything was created through him and for him. He existed before anything else, and he holds all creation together." – **Colossians 1:16-17 (NLT)**

> "So we look not at the things which are seen, but at the things which are unseen; for the things which are visible are temporal [just brief and fleeting], but the things which are invisible are everlasting and imperishable." – **2 Corinthians 4:18 (AMP)**

For decades, in this scientific and technological age, supernatural experiences and divine entities have been thought to be abstract from "reality." That's because these things can't be understood via protons, neutrons, and electrons. Yet, the ancients, including the Egyptians, Sumerians, Babylonians, Greeks, Romans, and others had entire cultures and civilizations centred on the supernatural, divine, and mystical. There were religious systems and hierarchies, along with protocols for ceremonies and rituals. These ancient human beings didn't hold their beliefs because they were deluded, but rather they saw the very *real* results of interfacing with the spiritual realm. Shamanism, spiritualism, ritualism, divination, and even animism, were all derived from these ancient peoples' spiritual practices (that continue to this present day). The diviners, oracles, priests, alchemists, shamans, and sorcerers of these ancient times interacted with the reality of the spiritual realm daily.

In this modern dispensation, many people through the influences of scientific theories and media culture, have come to regard the spiritual realm with a fictional or mythical lens. Through classic films such as *The Exorcist*, *The Craft*, and *Bewitched*, people have had their perspectives on the spiritual realm influenced by Hollywood, with often inaccurate depictions and representations of demons and witchcraft power. They have also been seduced through the media machine to desire spiritual interactions and exchanges *excluding* God. *Harry Potter* spawned a curiosity in the youth about witchcraft and spiritual matters, with many seeking occult/esoteric knowledge and participating in séances, Ouija board games, tarot cards, and psychic readings.

Mediumship and clairvoyance today can be accessed everywhere – from talk shows and other TV programming to online through social media psychic groups. Even law enforcement in the past few decades have used mediums to "solve" criminal cases. Western society in a matter of decades has gone from the influences of Edgar Cayce to Theresa Caputo (romanticizing psychic abilities while making a fortune). There's 'witch-tok' (witchcraft content communities on Tik-Tok), which is now growing rapidly, mainly with young adults and teenagers joining out of rebellion and curiosity. And global giant YouTube hosting 'World Tarot Day,' allowing the virtual reading of tarot cards on the Google-based platform.

Additionally, interest in visiting haunted houses and graveyards, and watching TV shows such as *Ghost Hunters*, *Paranormal Encounters*, and *Paranormal Investigators*, has sky-rocketed within the past few years – giving people their dose of spiritual (or ghostly) excitement. With all the fanaticism surrounding these disturbing trends and developments, people are not engaging in these demonic practices because "spirits or ghosts don't exist." They're participating in these spiritual activities because they're interacting with entities and realms that are very real and produce results.

The paranormal has increasingly become popular and normal in our society, yet the average Christian seems rather oblivious to it all. In 2009, a Barna survey found that 40% of Christians strongly agreed that Satan "is not a living being but is a symbol of evil," and 38% strongly agreed and 20% agreed somewhat that the Holy Spirit is "a symbol of God's power or presence but is not a living entity." These sad statistics make you wonder what the beliefs of average Christians are all these years later. We have Christians who say they believe in an invisible God (who is a Spirit), but they don't believe in the reality of other spiritual entities. They clearly either don't read or believe what the Bible says.

With all the war, hopelessness, brokenness, corruption, violence, terror, tragedy, and calamity that the world is constantly experiencing, it should be easy to discern that there is something else influencing these affairs. We are in a spiritual war with other spiritual beings. Some may call these spiritual beings Anunnaki, aliens, divine elements, spirit guides, energies, gods/goddesses, fallen angels, demons, Nephilim, and ancestors. But to the Christian, these spiritual entities are our enemies.

Throughout the scriptures, we can also see that much of Jesus Christ's ministry involved battling and overcoming these unseen enemies. In the New Testament, they are known as unclean spirits and devils. Jesus didn't ignore them and act as if they didn't exist – *he casted them out!* Not only did Jesus confront and combat these demonic forces, but he also trained his disciples how to deal with them and get the victory too.

In the gospels, Christ provides us with the perfect example for how to deal with our unseen enemies:

1. Pray
2. Fast
3. Confess the Word of God
4. Take authority and exercise dominion
5. Bind and loose
6. Lay hands when led by Holy Spirit
7. Expel and cast them out with assistance from Holy Spirit

God gives us an understanding of these unseen spiritual entities and how they operate in the Bible. We know according to John 10:10 that these spiritual beings seek to *"kill, steal, and destroy."* These entities kill people spiritually through enticing them to engage in sin repeatedly and unrepentantly; they steal people's God-given inheritance by diverting their destinies and frustrating them away from a godly path; and they destroy their prey through spiritual blindness and deception, which eventually leads their victims to hell. In Ephesians 6:12, Paul peels back the layers on these spiritual beings by revealing them to be principalities, powers, rulers of the darkness of this world, and spiritual wickedness in high places that are fighting against us. Apostle Paul further explains how to gain the victory against these entities by providing instructions in Ephesians 6:10-18. He expressed that the saints must put on the full armour of God and stand against the enemy.

Unfortunately, for some reason, many Christians are ignorant to the current spiritual warfare being waged and have not been engaging in battling the enemy. Instead, they appear to be in a spiritual stupor, allowing Satan and his cohorts to wreak havoc in their lives, homes, and churches. Yes, we are in a spiritual warfare! There is a reason why in Paul's second epistle to Timothy he referred to Believers as soldiers.

> "Endure suffering along with me, as a good soldier of Christ Jesus. Soldiers don't get tied up in the affairs of civilian life, for then they cannot please the officer who enlisted them." – **2 Timothy 2:3-4 (NLT)**

Soldiers are enlisted; they are trained, instructed in combat, and engage in battle and war against enemy forces. A good soldier will also be *knowledgeable* about their enemy. To have a winning advantage, a soldier should not and cannot afford to be ignorant about his adversaries and their tactics.

> "I have done this so that we may not be taken advantage of by Satan. For we are not ignorant of his schemes." – **2 Corinthians 2:11 (HCSB)**

> "Be sober [well balanced and self-disciplined], be alert

and cautious at all times. That enemy of yours, the devil, prowls around like a roaring lion [fiercely hungry], seeking someone to devour." – **1 Peter 5:8 (AMP)**

The Bible offers revelation about the devices the enemy seeks to use against Christ's soldiers. These include:
1. Demonic oppression and demonization
2. Seduction and demonic suggestion
3. Curses and cursed objects
4. Witchcraft and witches/sorcerers
5. Ungodly and demonic altars
6. Ungodly and demonic covenants
7. Soul ties

Since it would take another book alone to discuss all these things, I recommend reading the books *He Came to Set the Captives Free* and *Prepare for War* by Dr. Rebecca Brown, *Prayers That Rout Demons* by Apostle John Eckhardt, and *Deliverance from Demonic Covenants and Curses* by Rev. James A. Solomon.

My Warfare

"*Your destiny is in trouble,*" the Holy Spirit said with concern as I tried to get through my chromatography class. My professor was explaining our coursework in the lecture and reminding the class about our upcoming lab assignments. But I was in inner turmoil. Chemistry was the last thing on my frayed mind. The past year had been dreadful. A *nightmare* if you will.

After I said that prayer and had those dreams in my divine encounter with God (found in chapter 2), I began to struggle in a series of events that were draining me spiritually, physically, mentally, and emotionally.

It started when I went to bed one night in late December after my parents left from their visit with me. I laid on my mattress covered with fresh sheets, quietly preparing to get some sleep, when I felt like if someone was sitting on my bed.

I quickly sat up as I felt something touch my leg and then my thigh. Fear immediately sunk in as I realised…I was completely alone in my room. There was no other human there, and that's when it clicked what was happening. I opened my Bible on my nightstand and started praying until the weird feeling of panic left me. Whatever just happened was spiritual.

I tried to settle back to sleep but just as I was drifting off, my bed started to violently rattle and shake. This time I nearly jumped out of my nightgown as I got up to pray and then I started playing some prayers on YouTube I had found. Little did I know this would begin a trend of nonstop torment.

Another night I recalled being asleep and in and out of a dream but feeling as if someone was sexually prodding and caressing me in my private parts, sensing another *invisible presence* in my room. I even experienced evil spirits attempting to choke me, as I felt an entity's hands clasp around my throat and chest.

I entered the month of January 2018 haggard, and quite frankly, beaten up. Nearly every time I went to sleep, a few moments after I became consciously aware that I *couldn't move*. It was as if I was pinned down and something was sitting on top of me. However, each time I forced my mind and spirit to yell "JESUS," and once I did that, I was released. When I did my research, *sleep paralysis* was the term that popped up.

More frightening were the night terrors I was receiving. Imagine horror movies happening in your dreams nightly. I would see people being murdered in my dreams. I would see assailants try to attack me in my dreams. And, I would also have entities try to have sex with me in my dreams. Snakes, dragons, mermaids, witches, monsters, rats, cockroaches, dead people, and dead things. Anything unclean, awful, and distressing you could possibly envision was happening in high-definition when I went to sleep. I would wake up sweating profusely, but each time I would pray and ask God, or Yah, as I started to call Him, to cancel the effects of the dreams in Jesus' name.

By that time, I had learned about demonic covenants. I was led by the Holy Spirit to not only cancel my bad dreams out loud, but also to nullify any evil covenants I came into agreement with (knowingly or unknowingly) in the dreams.

However, no matter how much I prayed…things intensified.

If I wasn't experiencing sleep paralysis when I went to bed, then there was a spiritual force that slammed on my closet that drove me awake. I couldn't see anything physical that would cause the noise, but one night I saw the closet doors move on their own making the awful sound, and then God showed me I was dealing with a *poltergeist* spirit.

But that wasn't the only spirit I was encountering.

At night, I would see a snake hovering above my bed near the ceiling. It would move every time I was in and out of sleep, and its assignment was to clearly surveil me in the night. Years later, the Lord revealed to me that it was a marine or water snake spirit that was in my room.

Having all these incidents with the spiritual realm happen to me was absolutely terrifying and traumatic.

I can't forget about the witchcraft.

There was clearly an all-out assault on me. I was hyperaware that there were people that were trying to destroy me. This revelation again came to me in my dreams.

I had the experience of having a dream where I was at a witchcraft coven meeting with people looking at me. I woke up in shock, as I had never been a witch or involved myself in any rituals or occult ceremonies. I also remember seeing witches and warlocks in my dreams coming to attack or antagonize me, and they were nearly always dressed in black. Somehow, I was able to discern that they were evil spiritual agents, but more often than not I couldn't see their faces in the dreams. I would also see random people trying to make me eat in dreams, and worst of all, there was an attempt to kill me in a dream via a car bombing!

Then there was the witchcraft monitoring.

Something strange was happening with my apartment. On my room's side, there now always seemed to be a congregation of birds. This had never ever happened before, and even the next-door-neighbour tried to contact my landlord to see what could be done about the problem. There was bird poop and feathers scattered on the eastern side of the building. One day, I exited the apartment to make my way to class when perched right on the porch was the hugest crow I had ever seen! The crow was massive and cocked its head with its eyes staring directly into mine. It did that for a lengthy time before it moved off as I started to walk toward the bus stop with an eery feeling.

"*You're being watched, Camille*," said Holy Spirit as I stood at the bus stop. And it was true.

Whenever I started to pray, the birds would randomly smash into my bedroom window. I learnt quickly to keep my window closed. Birds would also follow me around my university's campus, and I would start praying until they eventually flew off.

God was showing me that the enemy was using these birds as monitoring spirits, sent on assignment to watch my every move and relay their findings back to their demonic headquarters. However, they weren't the only monitoring spirits being used by the enemy against me at that time. Flies en masse would enter my room buzzing constantly. I bought insect spray to kill them, but they seemed to resurrect and come back in even bigger groups until I realised that prayer would keep them away.

Because I was experiencing these things, I unfortunately took some bad advice from someone who I once trusted. They told me all I had to do is try to "meditate" and open my third eye, and then things wouldn't be so bad. Well, that turned out to be a lie.

One day, I was in my room and attempted to do what they suggested, when I was stopped in my tracks. In my peripheral I saw a dark shadow spirit man that had red gleaming eyes standing over me. When I turned and saw it in full view, I screamed "JESUS!" as this entity quickly disappeared right before me.

After this incident, God revealed to me that Christians are not supposed to meditate like people in eastern religions or open their third eye. Instead, Christians were only supposed to meditate upon the Word of God as stated in Joshua 1:8 and let God reveal things spiritually as he led us. He didn't have to tell me twice. I learned then to take people's advice with a grain of salt concerning my situation.

Things get *more* intense.

I started to notice that certain areas in my apartment would get bone-chillingly cold. There was no rhyme or reason for the occurrence, and the heating and cooling system in the building was not malfunctioning. The temperature imbalance in the apartment was ridiculous, yet none of my roommates seemed to notice anything wrong. The cold feeling in these areas along with the dark evil feeling emanating from them, were a stark contrast to the Holy Spirit's fire and comforting presence I had grown accustomed to. The dark evil presence seemed to intensify mostly at night and when I was alone in my room.

It got to a point that one night while I was trying to sleep, I opened my eyes to see an angel fighting a demon right over my bed! I had never seen anything like it. The angel seemed wrapped in a ball of pure light while the demon appeared wrapped in a black essence. The two were in an intense battle. Just imagine a black cat and a white cat scrapping and attacking each other in a flurry of hits and assaults. That's what it looked like. I couldn't see any distinct details of them like their countenance, armour, physique etc., but the Holy Spirit gave me the discernment to distinguish between them.

After seeing the angel and demon fighting, the Holy Spirit gave me awareness of angelic presence in my room when I was in serious times of praise and worship. I would see them appear in my room as lights, and whenever they were present, the demonic presence would evaporate.

The Lord was continuing to open my spiritual eyes, and I would even start to see demonic entities at my workplace. While on the job, the atmosphere would change in the office, and I would start to see demons looking at me while I worked behind the desk. These demons took the form of skeletons (think of the Grim Reaper from *The Grim Adventures of Billy & Mandy*) or dark shadows and black mist. This experience of course was unnerving, and I would have to act completely normal while on the clock until I could escape.

Even crazier was the demonic influence over my technology. Both my laptop and cell phone would go through periods of "spasms." Random text messages of gibberish were sent to me; weird words and different languages would pop-up when I attempted to communicate with others. It wasn't malware or a virus. I even bought myself a new cell phone assuming that my old one was on its last leg, but the same things would occur with that device. The Lord started to show me this wasn't normal, and that demonic spirits could manipulate and operate through the technology and devices we use in everyday life. It was just another level of demonic harassment, since I used my devices to play gospel music, prayers, and sermons.

Another problem persisted though. I started to have experiences where I would *feel* demons enter my body and consciousness. It started with hearing other voices that I knew were not my own or the still small voice of God. I would hear voices say, "I'm going to kill you!" or "I want you dead!" Then I would feel an entity physically enter my ear canal and start talking to me. When I would pray, to distract and discourage me, an entity would start screaming in my ear or cause a "buzzing" sound. Now some would call this experience tinnitus (a medical term for a constant ringing in the ear), but I knew this wasn't the case, because when I rebuked the "buzzing spirit" (as I'd come to call it) in the name of Jesus, the buzzing sound would stop.

As my dreams that ended in sleep paralysis continued, I would feel evil spirits "jump" into my body. I would start crying when this happened because it was completely against my will, and it seemed I was totally helpless to stop it. Not only would these entities enter my body, but I would hear them start to talk to me *internally* as well. I would hear these demons "announce" themselves, so to speak. Let me try to explain.

At this time, I was in terrible spiritual bondage. I had a strong spirit of condemnation. I couldn't bring myself to forgive myself for the sins I had committed in the past, and I kept beating myself up for doing those things. The spirit of condemnation would start saying, "condemnation, condemnation, condemnation…" repeatedly in my consciousness. The spirits of jealousy, perversion, despondency, depression, confusion, and rejection would also let me know that they were there by taunting me and telling me their names. It was the weirdest thing to me, as if these evil spirits had a superiority complex and they needed me to know that they were inhabiting me and my space.

Eventually I noticed that rebuking them in the name of Jesus and reciting scripture would get them to *shut up*. But not for long, as these voices got more and more aggressive and persistent, to the point where I couldn't distinguish the voice of the enemy versus the voice of God. During this time there was so much confusion, that the enemy did a great job of masking his voice as the Holy Spirit's voice.

One night in a fit of tormented weeping, I heard a voice say, "cut your hair!" At this time, I had locs and was being made to feel as if having this hairstyle was a sin. I thought I was hearing God, but it was really the voice of condemnation and confusion. I got up in the middle of the night, took a scissors and cut off my beautiful locs. Immediately after I did this, I heard a voice start cackling in a most evil way. It's the kind of wicked laugh that you only hear in horror movies. "You fool!" the voice said. I realised quickly that I'd been duped, which led me into another round of desperately crying.

There was non-stop torment occurring in my life during this season. I remember several times locking myself into my bedroom and crying, hearing voice after voice invading my space. To many around me, I seemed to match a psychiatric case perfectly. I had lost so much weight due to fasting and looked gaunt with a persistent sad countenance. I was a shadow and a shell of a human at this point. With all these things happening, it was a wonder I hadn't died.

Even in this desperate state, one day as I was in my room and I heard Holy Spirit say one word to me that kept me clinging on to life. "*Providence*," said Holy Spirit. It was him who was keeping me despite my circumstances, and that was his way of letting me know. Providence meant that he would provide me the spiritual care, grace, and guidance I needed to get out of this horrible situation.

MEETING A WITCH

To add to this spiritual onslaught, I would come face to face with a witch.

I was talented in music and would perform in my university's small town on and off campus (singing and playing the guitar). Because of this, people knew of me, and I had some measure of popularity. By chance (or not really), I met up with a female spoken word artist who regularly performed in the town's café and club circuit. She was Black and had Jamaican heritage. Somehow, she recognized me and asked for my contact information, because she was planning a Black History Month celebration show and wanted me to perform.

Because of the chaos in my life, I was accepting any opportunity to escape my unfortunate reality, and performing was just another escape, so I agreed to do it. Two days before I was slated to perform, this woman, who I'll call Bambi, wanted to see the set I prepared for the show. She called me and invited me over to her house. On arrival, everything in me screamed danger, but I still proceeded.

Inside the house could only be described as something out of a horror flick. There were shelves that had potions, herbs, and jars filled with magical ingredients. There were spell books, crystals, ancient grimoires, tarot cards, and other occult objects associated with magick all over the house. Every wall of the house had posters, artwork, and graffiti of occult symbols and witchcraft runes. There were also weird lights in the rooms and a diffuser that released a sickeningly smelling vapour into the air, that only added a further creepy effect to the already mystical and supernatural atmosphere. My eyes grew bigger with each thing I witnessed and saw. All I could do was quickly perform what I had planned for the show and make a fast exit.

I felt so dirty and unclean when I left Bambi's house, that I prayed all the way back home and took a shower immediately after returning. But showers don't get rid of evil spirits or curses. I knew exactly what Bambi was. And the thing that was scary is that I wouldn't have known if I didn't visit her home. Bambi was likeable, kind, and sociable. You would never think she was involved in witchcraft. Although I wanted to, it was too late to back out of the show, so I did it. And it was such a success that the event's story made it to the university's newspaper.

But there was something that happened the night we performed. It was a knowing of spiritual power versus spiritual power. I noticed that Bambi looked upset the entire time I performed (yet everyone else in the room was cheering me on – I gave a great performance). I personally believe God's presence showed up when I was singing because one of the songs was about him. Two or three acts later, in her spoken word set, Bambi in her poetic performance declared herself to be exactly what I knew she was – a witch – veiled under the guise of Black and female empowerment and liberation. Bambi knew what spiritual source she was tapping into; I knew which source I was tapping into, and the two were *not* the same.

A few weeks after, I learnt that she was the head of the Black Lives Matter chapter in my university's city. Bambi was trying to get students to join the chapter and was organizing BLM activism within the city. The reason why this is significant, is because BLM was founded by openly lesbian women who follow and practice *Ifa* and *Lucumi*. These are African Spirituality systems that involve divination, root work, spell work, and veneration of one's ancestors and orishas (West African pagan gods). The BLM founders are open about this fact, and they're also open about the necromancy involved when they pour out libations and give oblations to Black "fallen ancestors" or those whom they deem victims of White police brutality. These principles and this organization are what Bambi believed in.

It was after my interaction with Bambi that the battle raging against me reached its climax. I was targeted. Our enemy knows us (Christians) well and he sends his agents to do his bidding. What happened with Bambi was all planned. It was a trap and a ploy. Her job was to get close to me, close enough to harm me (I ended up having a dream about her too). But God had something to say about those plans, and he shielded me. Mysteriously, Bambi disappeared from my radar after the show. I never saw her again after that and nor did I want to.

With all this craziness going on, my parents were worried sick. And they had every right to be. They were seeing their daughter deteriorate right before their eyes. I tried to express some of what was going on to them, but they never seemed to fully get it – and how could they? What I was going through to someone who lacked spiritual discernment would've appeared as a clear-cut psychiatric case. But I wasn't crazy.

I was on a collision course with so many spiritual attacks. So, God was right – my destiny *was* in trouble. The enemy wanted to take me out before I could fully understand or realise who and what God called me to be. Something life-changing had to happen before it was too late. I got up from my lecture after it ended and made my way across campus to the bus stop.

I needed deliverance.

5 | THE DELIVERANCE

"How God anointed Jesus of Nazareth with the Holy Ghost and with power: who went about doing good, and healing all that were oppressed of the devil; for God was with him."
Acts 10:38

If you were trapped in a prison cell, bound hand and foot with chains, tormented daily, and in deep pain, would you want someone to rescue you? I bet you would. You would have every right to desire freedom, vindication, and even justice. That is what spiritual deliverance does. Deliverance releases a soul from bondage and then brings peace, love, and joy into one's life. And indeed, God has anointed and called his people to loosen the chains, destroy the yokes, break open the prison doors, and retrieve people from demonic cycles of brokenness.

> "The Spirit of the Lord is upon me, because he hath anointed me to preach the gospel to the poor; he hath sent me to heal the brokenhearted, to preach deliverance to the captives, and recovering of sight to the blind, to set at liberty them that are bruised, To proclaim the acceptable year of the LORD." **– Luke 4:18-19**

In this age of "churchian sensationalism" many have viewed

deliverance as just demons being cast out of someone. Some, who have purported themselves to be "deliverance ministers," have created an element of spectacle in the Church regarding the supernatural power of God to drive out evil spirits. Thus, a few of these "deliverance ministers" in their pride and need for attention, have posted videos online of them "delivering" people of demons and becoming agents of entertainment. This behaviour along with some obvious theatrics, have influenced many Believers and non-Believers alike to doubt the real power of God to destroy the works of the enemy.

As unfortunate as it is, much of the Church has considered deliverance to only be a "come out in Jesus' name" event. However, the Bible references many instances where deliverance (liberty) was gained from situations, relationships, harmful environments, and people.

There are two words I've found in scripture to mean deliverance in the Old and New Testaments:

> יָשַׁע - *yasha*: to deliver, save, avenge, help, preserve; to bring salvation or to gain the victory.
>
> ἐκβάλλω - *ekballó*: to drive out, to cast out, to expel, or to compel one to depart.

In the Bible, we see God employ both yasha and ekballó deliverance in various instances. YHWH performed a yasha deliverance through Moses' leadership as Israel was saved from slavery in Egypt. This same type of deliverance was given to Israel when they were at war with pagan nations and received victory, or when they were in the yoke of bondage from other nations and

God orchestrated their release from captivity. In this way, we see Israel being delivered from evil kings, oppressive environments or situations, and circumstances of bondage.

However, when Jesus came on the scene, things shifted a bit. While yasha deliverance still existed for God's people, he was offering them ekballó deliverance from evil spirits or devils. We see this type of deliverance in the ministry of Jesus Christ and the Apostles of the Early Church in scripture. Through these moments of ekballó deliverance in the New Testament, we understand that demonic spirits can cause sickness/infirmity, mental illness, disability, oppression, and more. These spirits were able to enter the people they inhabited because of sin, disobedience, rebellion, and generational iniquity. The unclean spirits were intelligent beings capable of having conversations and expressing spiritual knowledge, and they were able to negotiate and know who was anointed and appointed, and who was not.

Since becoming born-again, God has highlighted to me the severe importance of both types of deliverance. Particularly, the Church's participation in the latter type. Every Sunday, millions of people sit in church pews who are oppressed and demonized by evil spirits, and absolutely nothing is done about it. This should never happen, but it's also not surprising. Satan has done a good job of deceiving many Christians, who believe in cessationism and other erroneous doctrines, that casting out of demons, spiritual gifts, and some five-fold ministry offices only existed in Biblical times and aren't applicable today. A large majority of church leaders have gone to seminary and bible college but have not come to terms with the spiritual reality of this Christ-walk. Puffed up with their theological knowledge, exegetical prowess, and homiletical expression, they've never allowed God to show them certain things that would enable them to move in power and be effective in ministry through administering deliverance.

> "For the kingdom of God is not based on talk but on power." – **1 Corinthians 4:20 (AMP)**

On the other hand, there's been a recent resurgence and popularity of deliverance ministry in the Church, which has almost appeared cultish. There must be balance. Not everything that is going awry in a person's life is a demon. Some things are driven out of our lives by seasons of consecration, moments of divine revelation, good therapy, lifestyle changes, and truly getting into the Word of God. We also can't go around casting demons out of everyone either. There are some people who cannot and should not receive deliverance ministry because they either are not Christian or living a set apart life. If evil spirits were to be cast out of such people, the Bible tells us that those demons will return along with seven more evil spirits, leaving the individual in a worse condition than before (Matthew 12:43-45).

These things I know to be true of deliverance:

1. It is the children's bread and is accessible to the Believer.
2. It is conditional: repentance, renunciation, and breaking generational curses must be done for true freedom to occur.
3. It must be Holy Spirit-led. Trying to deliver someone without the leading of the Holy Spirit can lead to disastrous

results.

4. It must be maintained. Deliverance is maintained by continuing to keep spiritual doors closed to the enemy through living a lifestyle of holiness and repentance.
5. Deliverance is not a one-time event; it should happen multiple times throughout a Believer's life. Those in church leadership should be receiving regular deliverance since they have much spiritual warfare to contend with.
6. It is an act of God's mercy and love. We can thank God for the authority that comes with the name Jesus, and the power of Jesus' blood and the Holy Spirit.

There are great books you can read on the topic of deliverance. I recommend *Pigs in the Parlor* by Frank and Ida M. Hammond, *Deliverance and Spiritual Warfare Manual* by John Eckhardt, and *They Shall Expel Demons* by Derek Prince.

My Deliverance

MY DELIVERANCE

"Thank you!" I said to the bus driver as I hopped off at my stop. I was tired, but I managed to walk the few minutes it took to get to my student apartment. I took off my jacket, dropped my bag on the floor in my room, and then slammed myself into my bed.

At that moment, I felt so depleted and exhausted that I just laid there with my eyes closed, in a world of inner turmoil. Out of nowhere, I heard a voice echo inside of me. The voice was filled with care, concern, and urgency, and the voice started to pray for me. The prayer started in English, as the voice prayed for my healing and my future, and then the prayer continued in another language that I did not understand at rapid speed. The voice spent what seemed like around 5 minutes in total praying for me. As surprised as I was, I was too tired to react, and so I drifted off to sleep. It was the best sleep I'd had in months – no sleep paralysis, no demonic dreams, no weird spirits entering my room – it was peaceful.

This encounter happened a few short weeks after Holy Spirit had warned me that my destiny was in trouble. I was about to start my final year exams and was in a pitiful state. When I woke up, I remembered the voice that was praying just before I was asleep, and I wondered – who was praying for me? I was alone in my room! A shocking thought, an impression reached my mind: "*Me.*"

Perhaps I'm one of the few who've had such an experience. I literally with my own ears and inner man heard the Holy Spirit pray for me. It has been one of the most gracious experiences I've ever had to date. I've told this experience to people who've scoffed at me and called me silly or crazy (and these people were Christian).

To this day, God assures me that I wasn't crazy, and that what I just described actually happened. Here's the Bible to back that up:

> "Likewise the Spirit also helpeth our infirmities: for we know not what we should pray for as we ought: but the Spirit itself maketh intercession for us with groanings which cannot be uttered. And he that searcheth the hearts knoweth what *is* the mind of the Spirit, because he maketh intercession for the saints according to *the will of* God." – **Romans 8:26-27**

> "Therefore He is able also to save forever (completely, perfectly, for eternity) those who come to God through Him, since He always lives to intercede and intervene on their behalf [with God]." – **Hebrews 7:25 (AMP)**

God himself was interceding for me, and so were countless other people at the time, including my parents, Pastor A and his wife, and the Christians my mother were asking to pray for me. I needed to be rescued and freed, and prayer was just one of the steps.

My mother during this period contemplated coming to Canada to help me and was also asking me to return to Barbados ASAP. The part about me flying back to Barbados was problematic. I was getting constant visions of a plane crash and seeing myself in hell. These were obviously demonic, but with the mental state I was in, I was terrified to get on an airplane.

The enemy managed to deceive me about certain members of my local church and cornered me into a season of isolation where he was pummelling me. The demons were constantly toying with my mind, but God was the tether keeping me connected to sanity. I was fasting to get rid of these evil spirits with no victory, to a point and severity of vomiting up bile. I had lost tons of weight and looked like the epitome of death walking (death was actually at the door).

I even recall going to the city hospital to seek medical help for the pain I was feeling due to the fatigue and malnutrition. Only to have a doctor, who was also a shaman (he later revealed himself to be one), tell me, "You should stop fighting the demons at night. It won't help." I never told this man about the night terrors or demonic encounters I was experiencing. All I told him was that I was feeling ill. But through his occult gift, he was able to know what was happening to me and told me not to fight the entities that were afflicting me. I left that hospital in a hurry and never went back.

When I finally reached the sanctuary of Pastor A's home, I remember specifically feeling like if life was not worth living anymore. I wanted to die. To die must be surely better than this, I thought. But God wouldn't let my thoughts go too far down this line. While at Pastor A's, the Holy Spirit kept reminding me that he had called me and wanted to use me. My life was important to God, but I couldn't understand why. To me, there was nothing to live for with the constant attacks and misery.

I still didn't understand when I was on an airplane headed to Barbados after spending 5 weeks at Pastor A's either. On the train-ride to the airport, the Holy Spirit said to me, "*Everything will be all right. You'll be safe and no harm will come to you.*" The Lord knew I was still rather terrified of flying on a plane because of the demonic visions I was being bombarded with. But when He spoke those words to me, I was filled with a peace I couldn't understand. I made my way towards the gate, and guess what? No harm came to me on my flight.

When my mother laid eyes on me as I exited the arrival hall, all she could do was hug me. Every part of her face was the picture of concern – and who could blame her? Her first course of action was to get me eating properly again and she immediately made appointments for me to get my hair done and see a medical doctor. It was quite methodical what she did to get some semblance of her daughter back. The Holy Spirit was leading my mother whether she knew it or not. My Mom made a point of getting me out and about with family members, friends, and my godmother. She wanted me to get back to myself and offered me the normalcy of familiarity. However, I was still in utter torment, and she saw that very clearly.

Though bewildered, my mother also booked an appointment for me to see a psychiatrist I had talked with a few years previously. He was a gingerly and kind older gentleman, who listened to me patiently while I described some of what I was experiencing. Throughout the session though, I sensed I wasn't going to receive the help I needed from psychiatric intervention, so I said very little after this. That didn't stop this psychiatrist from prescribing me two medications – one for anxiety and the other for me to get sleep. When I got the medication, I didn't want to take it, since I felt it wouldn't help – and it didn't. In fact, one of the medications that was prescribed to me was also a popular drug for people experiencing schizophrenia and paranoia – neither of which I felt

I was personally suffering with. The psychiatrist did diagnose me with what he called *hyper-religiosity*, however. Despite taking the medication, I couldn't sleep properly due to being demonically attacked and harassed.

Since the psychiatric appointment still left the matter unresolved, my mother started to explain my situation to another co-worker of hers. This turned out to be a really good thing. My mother's co-worker, like me, had experienced similar unusual spiritual occurrences in her life. She was a born-again Christian and mother, who had to flee a foreign country and leave her marriage because of witchcraft and demonic entities severely attacking her. Her supernatural experiences were close in nature to mine, and she told my Mom her testimony of how God saved her. Because of her background, my Mom's co-worker was seeing a Christian counsellor and life coach, who was helping her with therapy as she navigated the aftermath. Not only did she recommend that my Mom allow me to see this Christian counsellor, but she also lent my mother a book on prayer, to learn how to strategically pray for me.

During this time, my godmother (who is a praying and God-fearing woman) also connected my mother to a pastor who she knew conducted deliverance. This pastor's church was located in my island's capital and was denominationally Pentecostal. I remember meeting up with him during a weekday service, and he prayed for me and told me I should get baptised. I agreed with his sentiments as I had long wanted to get baptised and couldn't do it in Canada. And so, myself and a small group of new Believers, got baptised by this same pastor on a Saturday afternoon by the beach. Both my mother and godmother witnessed me get baptised, and I was simply relieved that I finally had the chance to be fully born-again. The pastor instructed me to come to his church service the next day and he would provide me with deliverance ministry. It wasn't until I was in the church service that Sunday that I realised this pastor had no intention of conducting my deliverance. Instead, there was an entertainment piece I hadn't factored in.

Just after the sermon was preached by another minister, the pastor called me out of the congregation and started prophesying to me. Much of what he was prophesying aligned with what the Lord had been telling me while I was still in Canada. One of the things he prophesied about was the fact that I had eaten food that was tainted by witchcraft. I knew about this matter because the Holy Spirit had already revealed to me that someone close to me gave me food over which spells and curses were done. Eerily, before I even left my island to study in Canada, my godmother prayed for me and told me to be careful who I ate from. Her warning had come full circle. The second part of the pastor's prophetic word was that there was a warlock who had been attacking me who had come from under the sea. This too I also knew to be true, since this very thing was disclosed to me beforehand by Holy Spirit and my dreams were manifesting these attacks. To those who don't know, there are witches and warlocks who gain demonic powers from the waters (seas, rivers, lakes, etc). Some of these occultists even supernaturally travel and live under the sea, communing with fallen angels, mermaids, serpents, and

Nephilim. There are demonic kingdom networks, portals, and ley lines that interconnect water bodies supernaturally.

The pastor then called me up to the front of the church and started commanding demons to come out of me. In simple sorrow, I just burst into tears. The pastor and his congregants were looking at me to see if they would see some sort of demonic manifestation or reaction, and when that didn't happen, I was quickly ushered back to my seat and told that they would pray for me and that I would eventually get my deliverance.

Needless to say, I left that church with a holy anger. What happened to me should have never happened. I should have never been called up publicly in that manner to receive deliverance. After the service, my mother encouraged me to talk further with this pastor. His demeanour had changed, because now his attitude toward me was flippant. It seemed he no longer had any use for me. The care, love, and compassion of a deliverance minister was lacking in this pastor. I guarantee if the spirits causing havoc in my life had manifested in front of everyone that Sunday, the response from this pastor would've been different. I left his office and never spoke to him again. He nor his church ever followed up to see how I was doing or if I needed further assistance.

This mishap deliverance didn't stop God from getting me the freedom I needed. The Christian counsellor that my mother's co-worker recommended, who I'll call Minister Clarence, had been contacted by my parents and was told about my situation. I spoke with him briefly on a phone call they had one night, attempting to explain what was happening. He coordinated with my mother to pick me up and bring me to his home office for a counselling session. My mother attended the session with me. Minister Clarence was very kind and seemed genuinely concerned about me and what I was going through. He was also a wellness coach, and very big on wholistic healing and health (body, soul, and spirit from a Christian/biblical perspective). As soon as I walked into his office and sat down, I heard the Holy Spirit say, *"Talk. Talk to him."* And so, I did.

I started talking to Minister Clarence about my dreams, the demonic attacks, the witchcraft, the Holy Spirit encounters, the fasting, the shift in spiritual diet – everything. I even showed him one of my prayer and dream journals. At this point in the session, he had asked my mother to step outside so he could just hear from me. Once he was finished making some notes, he called her back into his office. "Ma'am, your daughter is not crazy. There is a reason why the enemy attacks certain people the way he's attacking Camille," he said.

Minister Clarence then went on to disciple me further, and some of the questions I had that others simply couldn't explain, he managed to answer in such a digestible way that I fully understood. He went on to organise with my mother to get me into a deliverance session, with him and another pastor, which he suggested would start to help me gain some freedom and healing.

Furthermore, Minister Clarence also set me up with a list of supplements, vitamins, and dietary ingredients that he urged my mother to start allowing me to take. He knew that my body was depleted and weak from the fasting and trauma, so he wanted to build my body back up with a good multi-vitamin, protein supplement, probiotics, and a healthy diet that would provide me with the nutrients I needed to get strong. Later, both my parents would drive me again to Minister Clarence's office, this time for my deliverance, which was free of charge. Minister Clarence and his pastor friend greeted my family and talked us through what was about to happen. My parents were privileged to see me set free, as they were allowed to be in the same room.

With worship music playing in the background, Minister Clarence and his friend opened in prayer. They prayed for me, my family, and themselves, asking the Holy Spirit to take control and protect them as they ministered to me. One by one they started to call out unclean spirits that were both operating on the inside and outside of me, and they all came out as commanded. At the same time as these two men of God were casting out these evil spirits, the Holy Spirit himself was walking me through what they were doing and comforting me as well.

Every time I heard Holy Spirit mention a demon's name, the men of God would call out the spirit and command it to leave in the name of Jesus. I walked through repentance of some areas of unforgiveness toward myself and others, and on and on it went. I could also hear the demons putting up a fight in my mind, and they attempted to torment me but couldn't. Most of the deliverance happened with ease, as I yawned, vomited (a thick yellowish substance mixed with blood), and wept – all of which were manifestations of these spirits being driven out. Most of the demons came out via tears which I found ironic, since during my warfare and tribulation, I would cry and cry non-stop.

It should be noted here, that while I was in my tribulation and experiencing spiritual warfare in Canada, I was led by the Holy Spirit to make a list of my own sins and the sins of my ancestors (that I knew of, and that God revealed to me). Not only did I make this list, but I verbally repented and renounced all of these personal and ancestral sins and iniquities. Also, I was led by the Holy Spirit to discard all cursed and unclean objects from my home and life, including books, jewelry, music, and even clothing. Therefore, during my deliverance session with Minister Clarence and his friend, a lot of the repenting and renunciation had already been completed on my own (being led by Holy Spirit). It was by God's design that I was fully prepared for my deliverance and was completely aware of what was going on.

After my deliverance was done, they prayed for me again and talked me through the process of aftercare, ensuring that I would maintain my newfound freedom. They asked the Holy Spirit to fill me up in all the empty spaces in my soul, body, and spirit, and they also prayed for all inner wounds to be healed. These two men of God further gave me scripture to study and meditate on as part of my aftercare instructions.

Simple, straightforward, caring, attentive, and effective. That was how I would describe my major deliverance. Despite the concern from Minister Clarence and the very few family members who were aware of what was happening in my life, I now had to prepare for my university graduation in just a week. The plan was for my parents and I to fly back together to celebrate the occasion.

In fact, the Lord himself was urging me to go back to Canada.

"*Camille, your ministry will not be in Barbados, but it will be in Canada. You need to go back,*" was what Holy Spirit said.

In between the end of my last semester and my return for my convocation, the Lord had orchestrated the second part of my deliverance. This was the *yasha* side of things he was dealing with. Before I had even travelled to Barbados at my parents' request, he had already told me it was about to happen – but I didn't completely understand at the time.

The LORD revealed to me that I would lose all the "friends" and acquaintances I had acquired while attending university. He said I wouldn't remain friends with them, and that I would actually be moving to a new city. He was right of course. Some of my closest "friends" at the time who I expected to show up for me, immediately stopped talking to me. No explanation, no confrontation, just simply ghosted. When I attempted to reach out to them, the response was either non-existent or frigid at best. People I knew, helped, and loved now treated me like if I was the scum of the earth. In addition, some of the church "family" I had gained in my university's town, now turned their back on me and one of them even tried to scam me and take advantage of my fragility during my recovery. There was so much rejection, hurt, and betrayal all at once, just after gaining my *ekballó* deliverance.

My parents stayed with me a little while after my graduation, as I hastily tried to look for work in my university's town but found nothing. My living situation was not stable, and God reminded me that he no longer wanted me to stay in that area and wanted me to move. In fact, two older women who I considered sisters in Christ, had organised to get me into an illegal rental agreement so they could make some quick cash at my expense. God intervened and told me I would have to move to a city 4 hours away where I had some family members.

At the same time, he showed me that one of the two "sisters in Christ" was jealous of me, while the other one simply wanted to use me. God also revealed that the friends I was losing were *not* my friends and that they would pull me away from a relationship with him through their influence in my life. In essence, God was delivering me from a place of familiarity (my university's town) that had become a prison and a reminder of so many unpleasant things, as well as from people with ill intentions toward me, my wellbeing, and spiritual development. God was providing me with a *yasha* deliverance.

However, nearly everyone I knew was telling me I should count my losses, return to Barbados, and do something with my life. But this was not what the Lord was telling me to do. Everything I was being instructed to do by the Holy Spirit went against what others were suggesting. I had no choice but to ignore what everyone else was saying, trust the Lord, and obey.

There was only one word to describe how I was feeling: broken. I made the move. I cut the ties. I continued in my training. I accepted my calling.

6 | THE CALLING

"Who hath saved us, and called *us* with an holy calling, not according to our works, but according to his own purpose and grace, which was given us in Christ Jesus before the world began."
2 Timothy 1:9

In this hour and in this season, God is calling his people forth. He is placing his anointing on the Chosen to put their hand to the plow and work in the Kingdom of God. Jesus Christ is calling men out of addictions; he's calling them out of perversion; he's calling them out of confusion; he's calling them out of idolatry; he's calling them out of graves and tombs.

Abba Yah is drawing men by his Holy Spirit unto himself, but he's also calling them to Kingdom purpose. God wants people to stand up and accept their calling because he wants to use them for his glory. But what is a calling?

There are 2 main words for *calling* in the Greek according to Strong's Concordance:

> 1. **(2821)** is **κλῆσις** or **klésis** (klay'-sis), which means *to call or invite* (people into the Kingdom of God through salvation found in Jesus Christ).

> 2. **(2822)** is κλητός or **klétos** (klay-tos'), which means *to be called or summoned* by God to a ministry office or salvation (divinely selected/appointed).

From these interpretations of the Greek words, we can define a <u>calling</u> as: **a divine invitation and summons to receive salvation and enter into the Kingdom of God by appointment; selected for a divine office/position in Christ Jesus.**

Our Heavenly Father is inviting people to pick up mantles for the Kingdom. Further along in Ephesians chapter 4, we see that God gave some people distinct (ministerial or office) callings and gifts. We are to operate in our calling and gifts for the good of the body of Christ and as a testimony of our God to the world.

> "Wherefore he saith, When he ascended up on high, he led captivity captive, and gave gifts unto men. And he gave some, apostles; and some, prophets; and some, evangelists; and some, pastors and teachers; For the perfecting of the saints, for the work of the ministry, for the edifying of the body of Christ: Till we all come in the unity of the faith, and of the knowledge of the Son of God, unto a perfect man, unto the measure of the stature of the fulness of Christ." – **Ephesians 4:8,11-13**

When God calls you, he is inviting you to accept the destiny he has for you in Christ that existed before the foundations of the earth were laid. He's inviting you to perform your God-given purpose by following him through his Holy Spirit. Those whom God is drawing by his Spirit into the Kingdom of God are being called to do God's work according to his will. But there is something deeper than being called. And that deeper thing is to be *chosen* by God.

Again, I'll reference the Greek via Strong's Concordance. Here's what I've found:

> **(1588)** is ἐκλεκτός or **eklektós** (ek-lek-tos'), which means to be *elected, selected, and/or chosen out* by God to provide special service unto Him (with additional connotations for pre-eminence or excellence as implied via Thayer's Greek Lexicon).

"For many are called, but few are **chosen**." – **Matthew 22:14** (emphasis mine)

We see from the above scripture in Matthew 22 that many are called in Christ to God's purpose, but there is a select few that are chosen to accomplish certain things in the Kingdom of God. There is also the inference here that those select few are *both* called and chosen.

I've put together a very generalized list of what both being called and chosen may look like.

How do I know God is calling me?
- You feel led to repent of your sins and seek salvation in Christ Jesus.
- You have an inner need to pursue the things of God.
- You grow a greater hunger for the Word of God.
- Your desire to pray increases and you gain capacity.
- You have a need to get to know God for yourself.
- You begin a sincere relationship with God (everyone's relationship with God looks different).
- You have a sense that there is something greater in life awaiting you.
- You start to understand more about your unique purpose.

On top of that…

How do I know I've been chosen?
- You go through certain things in your life that other Christians can't relate to.
- You have an intensive and aggressive spiritual training period developed by God to prepare you for the work he wants you to do.
- You discern and understand things other people simply don't.
- You are able to perceive the intentions and motivations of the people around you.
- You understand that God deals with you much differently than he deals with other people. God has a different standard for you compared to others – there are certain things other people can get away with that you would be heavily rebuked for.
- You become a spiritual diagnostician and surgeon.
- You are entrusted with certain information from God that other people will not have revealed to them.
- You are often misunderstood and seen as weird or the odd one out.
- You stand out in the crowd; you don't talk, move, or think like other people (even those who are in the body of Christ).
- Your path appears more difficult and trying than other individuals'. You tend to suffer more than other people.
- Your prayer and Bible study life increase dramatically.

Some like John the Baptist, Samson (the Judge of Israel), and Jeremiah are called and set apart from the womb as the Bible states. Others are called to the service of the Lord as children and as adults. Since the Lord does everything in a balanced and orderly manner – some are called to do small things for the Kingdom of God and others are called to do big things for the Kingdom of God. The Lord made both the small and great. What is evident according to the scriptures is that God does not hide his calling from his people, and he always places his mark upon his chosen. What is this mark? It is the anointing – God's stamp of approval – that breaks the yokes. As a matter of destiny, one should intentionally inquire of the Lord what one's calling and divine purpose is. God desires for us to know our purpose and understand our calling, and he will reveal these things to those that seek to know them.

My Calling

MY CALLING

It all goes back to my childhood. In chapter 2, I mentioned how I had small encounters with God before my big encounter with him and that I experienced episodes of demonic attack. I think it's important to give you an idea of what I was talking about, because it honestly fits in with how God revealed my calling to me after my deliverance.

As a little girl, my mother and godmother took me to a Christmas concert at a local Pentecostal church in Barbados. I was maybe about 5 or 6 years old. Mum enjoyed taking me to Christian events like this as a young child and it was a way for us to bond and get out of the house. From what my mother told me, after the concert finished, the pastor invited anyone who wanted to give their life to Christ to another section of the church for prayer. Moments later as my mother and godmother finished socializing and were ready to go home, they realised that I was missing. My Mom started looking for me worriedly, wondering where in the world I could have disappeared to. In a few minutes, they found me in a room in the church receiving prayer and giving my little heart to Jesus. Years later, my mother said she always pondered about this moment in my young life considering where I'm at today. That was just the beginning.

Around this same age, my mother and I travelled to the twin-island nation of Trinidad and Tobago. There, we stayed at a hotel while we explored various parts of the island with some friends and fellow travellers. However, my mother had made arrangements with a family friend (who was an associate of my father) to spend the latter days of our trip with them. While spending the last of our time at the hotel before moving on to stay at this family friend's house, a man arrived at the concierge desk seeking to speak with my mother. My Mom did not know this man, but he knew her name and the hotel we were staying at. It turns out this man was the boyfriend of the female family friend we were soon about to be lodging with. He came before our set departure date from the hotel to warn my mother. His warning was simple. The female family friend we were about to stay with was a full-fledged witch, involved with a West Indian stream of occultism known as Obeah.

Not only was she involved with an occultist group and witchcraft practices, but the man warned that this female family friend's intentions toward my mother and I were not pure, and that there were ulterior motives behind the invitation extended relationship-wise. Before he left from telling my mother these things, he asked her to not expose him or the fact that he revealed these things. Then he was gone, leaving my mother absolutely shook. Mom had no prior knowledge about what the man told her, but she also couldn't extend our stay at the hotel because other guests were expected after us and they were fully booked.

We eventually decided to stay with the family friend. Doing so turned out to be an interesting experience. Because of the man's warning, my mother was on high alert and very mindful about every move she made, especially knowing that she had me with her. There were attempts made by this family "friend" during our stay to get us to eat food from strange places. There were invitations made by this family "friend" to go up into the mountains to obtain "holy water" to bathe with. This woman's daughters were instructed not to use certain items in the fridge that were meant for me and my mother to use, but God protected us by exposing it, and so, my Mom was able to throw these items away. The Obeah woman also attempted to place cursed money into my mother's hand, but that was thwarted with some discernment and quick thinking by my Mom. As the Lord so quaintly put it when I reminisce on this incident in my life, "*The arrows didn't work.*"

A strange experience also happened at the woman's house where her two children and I encountered some direct demonic activity. We witnessed patio furniture without strong wind or provocation start to move around on its own and heard strange voices talking and calling to us. The problem with that was the fact that we were alone (…or so we thought). We all heard and witnessed this event and immediately ran under the bed in the guest room afraid. It so happened that both my mother and the Obeah woman were not in the house during this occurrence. But we all knew it was spiritual.

On the day that my Mom and I were going back to Barbados, the Obeah woman gave my mother a book. The name of this book was *Powers of the Psalms* by Anna Riva. At the time, my Mom did not know that this was a witchcraft book (using Biblical psalms as spells and curses). She was just so happy to be leaving and to escape the situation. When we returned to Barbados, my mother told my father of the strange experience. He then did some digging and found out that everything that my mother said was true. In fact, the Obeah woman's father was such a well-known sorcerer that some Bajans left Barbados and travelled to Trinidad to seek his spiritual assistance. God protected me and my Mom during this time, and I've come to realise it was connected to my calling. If my mother and I had been bewitched in another country, the chances are likely that I wouldn't be where I am today.

When I was around 15 years old, I was just about to start taking my first round of CXC CSEC examinations in secondary school. I had made a few friends while at school and would talk to them during lunch and other breaks. One day the topic of spirituality came up. It just so happened that one of my peers started talking about atheism. Hearing the young man talk about his lack of faith and belief in God caused something to lurch in my spirit and my mind started to come under torment.

You see my exposure to the Christian faith was one of the bedrock layers of my upbringing. Having that faith challenged as a teenager not only bothered me but also caused me to question God's existence for myself as well. Matters were only made worse as I was experiencing depression at this time in my life over the pressures of academia and not fitting in like I thought I should. During this time my mental health took a serious hit. I started crying constantly and would cry about going to hell.

My mother and father didn't know what to make of their tearful and bewildered teenaged daughter. I also found a little book of foundational bible scriptures in my parents' exhaustive library, and when I read the scriptures, I saw my sin staring right back at me. This led me into another fit of crying and my heart was pierced. At this time, I couldn't sleep by myself (if at all) and my Mom resorted to sleeping with me. What I couldn't tell her is that I was seeing demons in my dreams. One particular instance stood out to me where I woke up in the night from sleeping in my mother's bedroom. All around me in the room I could sense an intense demonic presence that sent chills up my spine. The atmosphere was so spooky that I looked for another room in the house to sleep in. When I managed to finally sleep, I had a dream of a horned demonic entity looking the very picture of evil staring at me. I woke up in a sweat and could not get back to sleep.

Somehow, I was still going to school but looked worn and tired all the time. My mother decided it was time to speak to a psychiatrist, and I had a counselling session. I was then prescribed anxiety medication and put on rest. My Mom also got a family member who was a Methodist priest to talk with me. To this day, I have no idea how I still aced my exams. In this season of terror, I got to understand and experience God's presence. A few months after this terrible ordeal I was somehow "back to normal". I had an inner knowing that God was near, ministering to me, and would ensure that everything was okay. There was an evident peace from God that I received while going through this period.

I knew there was more to God than I was being exposed to or told. So, after this experience, I began to ask questions about Jesus and why Christians celebrated certain holidays, why we prayed to Mary, why some people spoke in tongues at other denominational churches and Anglican Christians didn't. My parents and Sunday school teachers eventually decided to have an Anglican priest attempt to answer some of these questions, but I was never satisfied with their faulty rationales or biased convictions. I started attempting to read the Bible on my own, but some of the words and concepts were hard for me to understand. I just knew there had to be *more*.

Fast forward to mid-2018 before my major deliverance. I was a university student under spiritual siege. Learning what I had come to know during the past year of tribulation, made me seek out deliverance in the province's capital. I traveled to a church in the heart of this mega-city that was pastored by a mature Filipino man who I'll call Pastor Harry. This church had on their website that they provided deliverance and healing for those needing such from the Lord. When I finally arrived, I was welcomed warmly and ushered into a seat. The worship was awesome, and I still remember that the sermon was taken from Judges 6 discussing Gideon, one of the judges of Israel.

After the service concluded, Pastor Harry pulled me aside in the near empty church room to begin deliverance. Two intercessors were praying as the deliverance was led by Pastor Harry. The pastor started asking me about myself, my background, why I came for deliverance, and what my relationship with God was like. The session concluded with not one single demon being casted out of me, but I was prayed for and led through renunciations and forgiveness. Something strange occurred. Pastor Harry started to tell me what he was seeing in the spirit realm concerning me. I'll summarize what he said below:

- "You have a calling from God. Welcome to the body of

Christ."

- "God wants to use you for your calling, but you must be properly cleansed and purified first."
- "Start praying for others, especially for healing."
- "It's important for you to form a relationship with Jesus and to not fall victim to religion. More peace will come once I do this."
- "You shall become a mighty warrior of valour and be like Gideon (though afraid but bold)."

Other things were mentioned by Pastor Harry about my life being very chaotic at that time and my battle with depression and perversion. However, these other statements that he made had me pondering when I finally left the church to make my way home. In my session with him, he confirmed what my mother's coworker had initially stated before – that I had a calling and an anointing. In my crammed life at the time, I didn't know exactly what to make of it, but I knew I had to seek the matter out with the Lord.

It was only after my major deliverance and moving away from my university's town that the Lord truly started to open my eyes to everything regarding my calling. There was a reason why from childhood I was drawn to God and was able to see and hear in the spiritual realm. There was a reason the enemy was so devilishly incensed against me and attacking me on every side. I would cry out to God and ask him what sin I committed that was so egregious that I was going through what I was going through. I would spend hours in my apartment bedroom repenting over, and over, and over again – just crying my heart out and trying to understand. I nearly fasted myself to death trying to find the answer. And one day, God gave me a response.

"*You are anointed and talented, and that means trouble for them,*" said Holy Spirit.

Furthermore, the Lord said to me, "*You are a seer and a psalmist. You can see. And you know things. You're called. You're chosen. This is why they are attacking you.*"

In a loving and gentle voice, the Lord also said something I'll never forget –

"*Camille, it will cost you **everything**.*"

But I had come to love the Lord so much. I had become acquainted with his ways. I was slowly starting to form a deeper relationship with him. And I accepted everything that came with what he was purposing me to do. I accepted destiny.

The reason I had so much trouble understanding this concept of being called before, is that I wasn't perfect. I didn't know enough. Wasn't grounded enough. Didn't think much of myself. But God shifted my mindset completely around. He wasn't looking for perfect, he was looking to perfect me into the image of his Son daily. He knew I was unstable and not grounded, but he was willing to grow me into stability and strength. God also knew I didn't think much of myself but reassured me that he chose me for what he knew one day I would become, not where I was at in these most vulnerable moments. God is always looking ahead to the finished work, and he is a God that knows the end from the beginning.

Moving to a new city shifted everything for me. And because I had accepted the call, the Lord now needed to induct me into his training ground.

7 | THE TRAINING

"Shew me thy ways, O Lord; teach me thy paths."
Psalm 25:4

Everyone who is called by God must be trained to be used by him. It doesn't matter whether you've been called as a five-fold minister, intercessor, elder, deacon etc. You must be properly trained and equipped. Those whom God has called to ministry must also be specially trained in alignment with their specific mantle. For example, a prophet or apostle will not be trained in the same manner as an evangelist or teacher. Not every minister or Christian for that matter has the same calling, grace, gifting, or skillset. Therefore, they must be trained to function in their own specific calling or office. A huge part of this training is often referred to as *'the wilderness season.'*

I have never known a man or woman of God who has been authentically and effectively used by God that hasn't gone through a wilderness season. The wilderness season often places a distinction between those who've been simply called versus those God has uniquely chosen. It's in the wilderness that greatness is birthed, character is built, revelation is released, power is administered, rank is obtained, yokes are broken, and God is glorified.

You can easily tell who hasn't been through a wilderness season. The wilderness is a season and place of processing that totally prepares someone to move in their calling and God-ordained purpose. You'll see those that haven't been through the wilderness, or have left it prematurely, often operating outside of their calling, ineffectively functioning, compromised, lacking integrity, seeking validation from men, and wanting to be seen and heard. Those who've been through the wilderness leave it with a different mindset – it's all God or nothing, it's his way or nothing, it's submission and yielding or it's destruction.

Some don't make it through the wilderness. They simply can't handle all that's being thrown at them, so they give up. Some are broken by it. Some are grieved by it. But some, after it is complete, thrive because of it.

The wilderness is often a lonely place to be, but those who go through it are _not_ alone – God is always with them. The loneliness of it is mostly because many people refuse go through it and so few understand it. In the wilderness, you are stripped of everything, crushed, and then put back together in a transformed, renewed, and better image of God and Jesus Christ.

WILDERNESS SEASON CHARACTERISTICS

1. **It's just you and God.** Other people simply won't understand you or why you make certain decisions, and there will be much rejection. God will drive a wedge between you and them so that he can create a relationship between *you and him*. This

results in deeper intimacy with the Lord.

2. **You become acquainted with the constant comfort of the Holy Spirit.** You'll need it because of some of the situations you'll find yourself in.

3. **Prayer, praise, and worship become your lifelines.** You won't survive without them, so they'll start to ooze out of you after a period of squeezing. Thanksgiving and praise will become as easy as breathing – it just has to.

4. **You are stripped of old ways of thinking, old habits, and outdated operations.** Holy Spirit will give you new modes and perspectives and will constantly challenge your negative attitudes (it's the only way to build Godly character).

5. **You endure pressure, pain, and suffering.** (Remember what I said in Chapter 3: The Tribulation). Pain, suffering, and pressure, produce diamonds in the rough. Your heart becomes tender, and you become more vulnerable and run to your Heavenly Father. You learn so much because of these things, and you share in the sufferings of Christ as we're told we must do.

6. **There will be intense training in spiritual matters.** A diet of in-depth Bible study and reading books from other Christians versed in specific topics. Spiritual warfare will arise, just so the Lord can train you how to fight demonic entities and evil practitioners.

Jesus is the ultimate example of this since he went through his own wilderness. In Luke and Matthew chapter 4, we see Jesus Christ coming forth from his baptism by John and being driven into the wilderness by the Holy Spirit, where he stayed for 40 days and nights. During this time, Satan came to tempt Jesus, but our Saviour rebuffed The Adversary each time. From Jesus' example, we can note some keys to overcoming and surviving the wilderness season.

JESUS' EXAMPLE – 3 KEYS TO SURVIVING WILDERNESS SEASON

1. Being led by the Holy Spirit – "Then was Jesus led up of the Spirit into the wilderness to be tempted of the devil...." – **Matthew 4:1**
2. Fasting and prayer (for power, consecration, to hear from Father God) – "...And in those days he did eat nothing: and when they were ended, he afterward hungered." – **Luke 4:2**
3. Reliance and confession in faith of God's Word – "But he answered and said, It is written, Man shall not live by bread alone, but by every word that proceedeth out of the mouth of God." – **Matthew 4:4**

Adhering to these keys will lead to the same spiritual result Jesus had:

"And Jesus returned in the power of the Spirit into Galilee: and there went out a fame of him through all the region round about." – **Luke 4:14**

God takes us through the wilderness and trains us in order to use us to teach, preach, exhort, prophesy, cast out demons, edify, and become a light for him in the midst of a dark and dying world. The Word of God makes this clear through Jesus' example of mentorship and discipleship to his followers.

Jesus trained his disciples to:

1. Pray (Matthew 6:9-13)
2. Cast out demons and heal the sick (Matthew 12:43-45; Mark 9:29; Matthew 10:1)
3. Understand God's Word [through parables and teachings] (Matthew 5,6; Luke 16)
4. Navigate spiritual warfare (Luke 10:19-20; Matthew 16:18-19)
5. Evangelise (Luke 10:1-12)

The Lord's people must be trained for the work of the Kingdom of God. Our Heavenly Father desires imperfect but willing people to raise up and use, because that's how he gets the greatest glory. Here are some areas every Believer will be trained on:

1. Hearing and knowing God's voice.
2. Prayer strategies.
3. Learning and practicing spiritual gifts.
4. Knowing and applying God's Word.
5. How to use spiritual weapons in spiritual warfare (wrestling the demonic).
6. Discerning between good and evil.
7. Keeping the flesh under subjection.
8. How to endure and be refined by suffering.
9. How to love others (Christians and Non-Christians) through the eyes and heart of God.
10. How to destroy the plans of the enemy and establish the

plans and will of God.

Training is preparation for what's to come. And, even when one passes through the initial training stages, God will continue to prune his seasoned servants and train them in new areas yet still. Many men want the glory of the Kingdom without going through the preparation for it. Don't be eager to skip God's training. Even soldiers (which we are in Christ) have to go through something called 'basic training,' where they learn the fundamentals of military life, procedures, and operations. God is our General and he wants to train and properly equip his people for the work he's called them to. And guess what? Each person's training looks different and can last different amounts of time.

My Training

My own wilderness season started after my major deliverance and university convocation. There was and still is a lot of processing that God is doing in my life. I'll share some of the areas God started to train me in.

HEARING GOD'S VOICE

As I mentioned in the previous chapters, God had me move out of my alma mater's town and to a new city. The Holy Spirit revealed exactly which city he wanted me to move to, and I obeyed. Now, even while I was under spiritual attack, I was hearing God's voice and became aware of when he was speaking to me. As I mentioned previously, the enemy had started to mask his voice to mimic the Holy Spirit's voice to deceive me. After my major deliverance, the Lord began training me on how to discern his voice versus the enemy's voice. God showed me that his voice and instructions would never go against his written Word. Therefore, it became my duty and responsibility to devour as much of God's Word as I could.

I took time to study the Bible, meditate on it, and memorize it. By doing so, I had something to fight the enemy's deceptions with. In between trying to find a job and building back my life in the new city, I was always reading and studying the Bible or listening to sermons that expounded on God's Word. In this way God started to speak to me via the written Word. Then I would pray using the scriptures to echo his Word back to him so that it would be accomplished in my life.

Once God had me filled up with the *logos* Word (written Word aka Bible), he started to strengthen me in the area of his *rhema*

Word (God's spoken Word). Father needed to show me all of the ways he talks to me. I knew he spoke to me in dreams, and I also knew I had the ability to audibly hear him as well. While other Christians I met had visions from God, I had a strong ability to *hear* him. Not only could I audibly hear Holy Spirit, but he allowed me to detect the nuances and changes in his tone, emotions, and moods concerning myself, environments, other people, situations, and events. Because I could hear him, I started to develop a type of prayer mode I like to call "conversational prayer". The Bible instructs us to –

"Pray without ceasing." – **1 Thessalonians 5:17**

We hear this scripture mentioned in the Church often, but rarely do we ever receive an explanation for how to achieve this. The key to praying without ceasing is to invite Jesus into your *thought life*. I learnt quickly that God cares about the minutiae of our lives. He wants to be included in our planning and invited to our meals. He wants to watch movies and TV shows with us; be around us while we complete our chores or menial tasks, and to help us in our conversations with other people. With this in mind, I started to ask God questions about any and everything and I was shocked at how quickly he would speak and respond to me. Sometimes I would hear him so crystal clear that it was as if he were standing or sitting right next to me in the room like a family member or friend.

I would see people while out shopping and after sensing certain things about their lives, I would ask God about them, and he would reveal things about them and then I'd pray and ask him to help them. I'd even crack jokes in my mind and hear Holy Spirit respond with a bout of laughing and he'd call me "silly." Yes, God laughs when we're being funny – it's in his nature to take pleasure in his creation (and comedy was created by him too). Often, I would wake up from sleeping and simply ask, "Father, how are you doing?" And he'd respond, "*We're doing good. How are you feeling?*"

Because of the auditory gift God had given me to hear him, he began a program for me to discern his voice from the enemy's voice. After my major deliverance, I was still being bombarded with mental attacks from the enemy. Whenever a thought or idea would enter my consciousness, Holy Spirit would follow up with the source of these thoughts and ideas and would challenge me as to whether it aligned with the word of God or not. Father was having me walk out the principles outlined in 2 Corinthians 10:3-5.

For example, the enemy was still attacking me with condemnation. Sometimes after I made a mistake, I would hear thoughts that would beat myself up. Holy Spirit would then follow-up with "*condemnation.*" He was telling me what spirit was speaking to me and that the thoughts were demonic, that way I could rebuke those thoughts and come in alignment with scripture (Romans 8:1) which says, "there is therefore now no condemnation to them which are in Christ Jesus…I am not condemned in Christ." God would give me discernment as to whether ideas or thoughts were coming from my mind, my flesh, demons, or the Holy Spirit.

Additionally, I found that God liked to speak to me in things that I enjoyed doing or through things I liked to engage with. I *love* music, so God would speak to me through worship or praise music

— he would communicate with me through lyrics, harmonies, melodies, and rhythms. I *love* reading and learning new things, so God would start speaking to me through Christian books, news stories, and other published articles. I *love* watching documentaries and films, and so he would start talking to me through actors' characters and YouTube videos. Do you see what I mean? God forms modes of communication with his children based on their unique needs, personalities, and interests.

The best part of this auditory gift was when I spoke with other people. When I was in conversations with family members, coworkers, church members, or strangers, God was present in those talks too. When I would say something to uplift or encourage another person, Holy Spirit would say "*happy*" to convey the emotion he was feeling concerning what was said or the seed that was planted. There were also several times when I was having conversations with others and Holy Spirit would reveal that they were lying or that a demonic spirit was speaking through them and not the actual person.

I realised that the more time I spent with God, the more I came to know and trust his voice. Like the Bible says –

> "My sheep hear my voice, and I know them, and they follow me: and I give unto them eternal life; and they shall never perish, neither shall any man pluck them out of my hand." – **John 10:27-28**

DISCERNING BETWEEN GOOD AND EVIL

I learned that one of my strongest gifts is the ability to discern and perceive things about people, places, and situations. It comes as no surprise because I had this gift since I was a child. The gift of discernment only intensified, sharpened, and took a more spiritual route when I dedicated my life to Christ and got filled with the Holy Spirit. Somehow, I would just "know" when people were being disingenuous. I could just "tell" when demons were influencing a situation. And I just "knew" when a "minister" was operating in divination or falsehood in ministry.

Before my deliverance, I had made acquaintance with a Barbadian minister whose prayer group I joined because of my mother. The prayer ministry was further overseen by the minister's spiritual father and apostle. I continued to keep up with the ministry after my deliverance too. At first, I was enjoying the prayer sessions and ministrations. I would join over Zoom or when I went back to Barbados to visit, I would go in-person. However, when I had moved, I started to notice things that didn't sit well with me with the leadership of the group.

I noticed how this minister only preached messages surrounding prosperity. I saw how he would snap at people who questioned his opinions or thoughts (even if the person questioning him backed up their views with the Bible). I watched as this minister seemed surrounded by people who had a Jezebelic influence over him. I observed how money was collected for the ministry and not used for the purposes it was given. I saw the spiritual plagiarism as this minister would take content curated by other well-known ministers, and post or publish them as his own material (without giving credit to the source). And there is much more I noticed that I can't mention here.

All of these things I pondered. One night after the prayer group meeting over Zoom, I decided to pray for this minister and the ministry. Surprisingly, the Lord started to talk back to me and further exposed certain things about the minister and ministry. I decided to share some of these things with the minister, but I was swiftly dismissed and told I was a "young Christian" and didn't know what I was talking about. Looking back, I probably shouldn't have said anything, but there was a feeling I couldn't shake (and one that I couldn't totally explain). I took the dismissal with humility and still continued to pray concerning what the Lord showed me. Other members of the prayer group began noticing many of the same things I did. The difference was that none of them were willing to say anything. I decided to leave the group.

About 2 years later, it was revealed that there was a major rift between this minister, his spiritual father, and some of the ministry's influencers. The division resulted in the ministry collapsing, contentions between members, and a breaking away between the minister and the apostle. Moves were made, and this promising minister no longer participated actively in ministry as he once did to my knowledge (as of the writing of this book).

I took the above ordeal hard. I had to learn from the Lord that not everyone in Christian ministry is actually living right and doing ministry for the right reasons. Ministry is not a game, and character as ministers of God matters to our Heavenly Father. The above situation highlighted my gift of discernment at work. It's the little things that people tend to overlook, but it was the little things that I always seemed to notice.

While searching for a job in my new city, I stayed with a relative of mine who I'll call Kaycee. Holy Spirit was the one who directed me to stay at Kaycee's house considering she was a relation on my mother's side. I was still physically weak and in pain post-deliverance, but I knew I needed to stay in Canada as per the Lord's direction. This was an opportunity to get myself together and learn what direction God wanted me to move in. My mother was not as happy with the living situation because of Kaycee's past behaviour towards her and other family members. However, Holy Spirit said Kaycee's house was the place to be for that season. Looking back, I can see why Father wanted me to stay with this relative. This period showed my acute discernment and exposed so much of the underbelly of my familial relationships.

Kaycee was older than my mother and had her own grown children. When I arrived in the city with my parents still with me, she willingly agreed to host me and outwardly seemed "happy to help." However, what transpired after my parents left to return to Barbados was interesting. Kaycee and her daughter would start monitoring my movements. They always wanted to know where I was going or what I was planning to do. They invited me around some of their church members and friends who always seemed more updated on my life than I was myself. I would notice negative comments veiled as "compliments" being shot my way. They would talk about the way I dressed or my demeanour, not knowing the horrid events that occurred to me just months before (my mother absolutely <u>refused</u> to let them know what really happened to me, they only knew I graduated university and was told I was recovering from an "illness"). They would gang together and speak disparagingly of me while I was still in earshot.

I was told stories by Kaycee about various family members (usually always painting these family members in a negative light), and the stories always involved her being some sort of saviour or knowing what was best for everyone. From these stories, the Lord showed me that Kaycee had deep-rooted bitterness, unforgiveness, resentment, and pride. Many a time as she was talking, I could identify these spirits operating in her life. Kaycee always needed to control the narrative and make herself and her immediate family appear in good standing. She was mostly condescending to everyone and rarely had a nice word to say.

When I landed my first job post-graduation, Kaycee attempted to sabotage me accessing some of the paperwork I needed to start employment. The job was part-time when I got it, but she scoffed and belittled me improving myself. When I started working, I offered to pay for some bills in the house and my mother also sent some money, but Kaycee refused to take anything. I learned quickly to stay in my room – it was literally my only refuge for peace. The comments were that I was anti-social and didn't like Black people (even though I'm Black of Afro-Caribbean heritage), but that wasn't the case. God was telling me to keep quiet and stay out of the way. Since I wasn't looking for hand-outs from anyone, I also picked up another job so I could save money to get my own apartment. The monitoring in the house got so bad that I would have to schedule phone conversations with my parents when I was at work or commuting, that way Kaycee couldn't try to listen in.

Since I wasn't telling Kaycee or her family what my plans were or having phone conversations with my family in the house, I noticed frustration and anger in Kaycee. She even boldly told my mother that she could "never get any information from Camille." But it was Father who told me not to say anything. Therefore, her and her family's demons would start to manifest. One night, Kaycee was having a phone conversation in the kitchen with one of her friends, and I entered to get something to drink. Well, Kaycee watched me the entire time and then she started to tell me something, but when I turned around, I wasn't seeing Kaycee talking to me. Instead, there was a devilish look on her face like an evil smirk as she turned her head to the side. I looked at the demon, responded quickly, and went back into my room. When I asked the Lord, "what was that?" Father simply replied, *"those demons want you to know that they're there."* Kaycee's daughter would soon start to have this same demon manifest on her face when she talked to me too.

God showed me that the spirits of Jezebel, Ahab, pride, witchcraft, lying, deception, slander, jealousy, and idolatry were at work in this family and home. No wonder the demons were manifesting so brazenly. No wonder the Kaycee didn't seem to like it when I would pray, worship, or go to church, while commenting that her own children seemed to have no interest in such things. All the Lord would tell me is, *"Camille, Kaycee can see the anointing on you."*

Everything would culminate to me eventually leaving. You see, people often show "kindness" without really being kind. Was Kaycee showing me a kindness by letting me stay under her roof?

Yes. But letting me stay under her roof while being petty, speaking negatively about me with her family, talking badly about other family members to me, and making underhanded comments wasn't kind either. I could see plain as day the evil that was in her heart, but the worst part was that she believed the lies coming out of her own mouth. I wasn't necessarily being mistreated (my mother told me if anything of the sort happened to return to Barbados straight away), but I wasn't being treated right either. Can you see the dilemma? Someone can do nice things for a person and still want a world of evil and misery for them too.

I didn't realise how much I was carrying emotionally from being in this situation, until I started to develop an unbearable pain in my right shoulder and upper back. The pain intensified every day for nearly a week before I literally began crying to the Lord in prayer. I sensed that the pain was of a spiritual origin. When I asked Father why my back and shoulder were hurting me so much, the Lord's answer was simple. "*The spirit of hurt is lodged in your back,*" said Holy Spirit. Then came the silence as I pondered what he told me. The hostile environment I was in, caused emotional hurt and pain which allowed a spirit to enter my body to manifest physical pain. I immediately started to repent, renounce, break curses, and then commanded the spirit of hurt to come out of me. When I did this, I literally felt this demon dislodge from my back and come out of me with a shudder. I began to thank and praise God because the pain I was feeling was totally gone.

I tried to save every penny as fast as I could, but an uncle of mine who learned what was going on sent me first and last month's rent money for an apartment. It was a God send. All I needed was to find a suitable place. Eventually, all the things I was discerning were exposed and confirmed in a dream. God is a God who justifies his people. I managed to leave under Kaycee's roof without uttering a bad word about her, without any hatred or unforgiveness in my heart toward her or her family. Living at Kaycee's was to help me sharpen my gift of discernment so God could further show me some people's intentions, demonic motivations, and how to navigate what I was discerning.

PRAYER STRATEGIES

Prayer is the lifeblood of the Christian. It's how we are able to connect with God, obtain destiny, and have the victory over the enemy. Truly, I started learning how to pray before my deliverance. I had read books by Derek Prince and Apostle John Eckhardt on prayer that helped to shape and further develop my prayer life. Because I was studying the Word of God so much, I was able to learn that God loves it when we echo back his Word to him in the place of prayer. And so, I started to pray the Word of God back to my Father concerning myself and others. I began to see instantaneous results.

I also came into an understanding that God hears and responds to what some consider the most trivial of prayers. For example, post-deliverance I was working two jobs in the new city. I would work a shift at one job and then leave shift to work at the other job. One particular day I was feeling so exhausted finishing a shift at my part-time work and dreaded going to my full-time job. While finishing up my night shift, I began to pray and tell God that if only

I didn't have to do any real work until 12 pm at my other job and could rest a bit that day, that I would be so happy.

When I left shift to commute to my other job, I arrived to the news that all the network and computer systems were down, and I would not be required to do much and still get paid. I was able to get some much-needed rest, and exactly at 12 pm, all the network and computer systems were back up and running. When I saw this happen, the only thing I could do was smile. My colleagues at the time couldn't understand why there was network trouble in the first place. But one of my then co-workers who was a Believer in Christ looked at me from across her desk and by discernment said, "this is happening because of you." I just grinned, knowing that God answered a simple prayer.

I understood how serious prayer was when I was in a tough living situation and having contentions with a demonized landlord who I was renting from. This particular landlord was making my life a living hell despite the fact that I paid my rent on time, minded my business, and just wanted a peaceable place to live. What I couldn't understand about this situation, was that the Lord gave me permission and instructed me to move into this particular rental unit. *Why on earth would you tell me to move here*, I thought. However, the Lord made it clear to me that I was in a season of testing, training, and fortification that could only come through a period of spiritual warfare, i.e. the landlord's wickedness.

I remember praying my little heart out one night asking God to move on my behalf and to vindicate me. I was confessing the psalms and praying God's Word back to him concerning his promises for my wellbeing and future. After praying, I looked up to see an angel darting away out of my room on assignment concerning my prayer. I didn't expect to see the angel, but the Lord allowed me to see. Within four weeks I was out of that apartment and moving into a better one. God answered my prayers, and he sent his angel on assignment to move on my behalf. In fact, this is what angels do – they respond to the Word of God and are sent on missions as God answers our prayers.

> "Bless the Lord, you His angels, You mighty ones who do His commandments, Obeying the voice of His word! Bless the Lord, all you His hosts, You who serve Him and do His will." – **Psalms 103:20-21 (AMP)**

Prayer is powerful. It is so potent when a prayer is issued from a pure heart and with godly intentions. And for this reason, God will instruct a righteous Believer to pray for others in order to snatch them out the fire.

> "...The effectual fervent prayer of a righteous man availeth much." – **James 5:16**

There was a weekend when I received a call from a family friend who was also a Believer in Jesus. She told me that she had been praying for me when the Lord began to tell her about one of my family members. She relayed that there was a need to keep this particular family member in prayer, as what she saw and heard was not good. After the phone conversation with this sister in Christ, one night I went to sleep and had a dream about the family member (who lived in Barbados).

In the dream I entered the Queen Elizabeth Hospital (in Barbados) and made my way to the ward where this sick

family member was being cared for. On arrival at the ward, it was pronounced that this family member had died. I was then transported in the dream realm to this same family member's funeral at a church. I saw a book of condolences open before me, and I wrote in the book the word "sad." The dream ended.

When I woke up from the dream the Lord began to speak to me. The Lord revealed that this family member had an illness that the enemy wanted to use to cause them to die before their appointed time. Because this family member was in sin and not right with the Lord, if they died, they would go to hell. Holy Spirit also revealed to me that this family member knew about Jesus, but didn't *know* Jesus, and God had given them multiple times to repent and get right. The Lord was not pleased. Yet, God still instructed me to pray for this family member. It is written:

> "Say unto them, As I live, saith the Lord GOD, I have no pleasure in the death of the wicked; but that the wicked turn from his way and live: turn ye, turn ye from your evil ways; for why will ye die, O house of Israel?" – **Ezekiel 33:11**

God said that he did not want this family member to die prematurely and be sent into the fire. So, Holy Spirit pressed upon me to pray and fast. The Lord said, *"I will hear you when you pray for [the family member]."* God revealed that he loved this family member very much and wanted them to repent, be saved, and know him. However, this family member was blinded by pride, stubbornness, alcoholism, recklessness, religion, and had curses attached to them which invited spirits of infirmity and premature death into their life.

When I told this person and other family members about the dream and the need for this family member to repent, I was initially dismissed and told I was being negative. Interestingly, God decided to speak again. The family member went to a church meeting, and it was prophesied that they had the spirit of death and infirmity hanging over them, and the man of God saw in the spirit this family member's spouse becoming a widow. I was contacted back in Canada and told what was prophesied and my response was simple: we need to pray.

I got to work. I prayed, fasted, and preached the Word to this family member. I began to have dreams that confirmed that my prayers were being answered. I also had dreams that confirmed that the strategy of the enemy was to destroy this family member via demonic gangs that wanted to fully infiltrate and overtake this person. When the family member needed to go in for their final medical procedure, again I prayed. A peace came over me and I knew that they would come out of the woods – and they did. The procedure was a complete success; the healing process was smooth – and guess what? – that family member is still alive today trying to build a better relationship with the Lord. To this day concerning my family, God still upholds his promise to me in Acts 16:31. I give Yeshua all the glory.

By praying for others, my prophetic gifting was revealed more and more. I would sleep and have dreams about politicians, celebrities, religious figures, preachers, other family members, nations, and secret societies. The instructions after waking up were simply to pray. This allowed me to step into prophetic intercession.

Prophetic intercession led to words of wisdom, words of knowledge, and prophecy coming forth (which I made a record of). The Lord would talk to me concerning Canada and Barbados and he would tell me to pray. God would show me in dreams preachers who were in secret occult organizations and operating via familiar spirits and deception, and he would have me pray for the people who were held captive in these false ministries. God made it clear to me that there was an anointing on my life for interceding for his people.

As much as I enjoyed praying for people and was being led to do this more and more on account of my gift, I had the shock of my life when God instructed me to *not* pray for certain people. The principle of not praying for some people was not one that was taught to me church, but I was educated about this matter in the school of the Spirit. Let me say this, it is *absolutely biblical* to not pray for certain persons. Don't believe me? Check out these scriptures:

"Therefore pray not thou for this people, neither lift up cry nor prayer for them, neither make intercession to me: for I will not hear thee." – **Jeremiah 7:16**

"Therefore pray not thou for this people, neither lift up a cry or prayer for them: for I will not hear *them* in the time that they cry unto me for their trouble." – **Jeremiah 11:14**

"Then said the LORD unto me, Pray not for this people for their good." – **Jeremiah 14:11**

Father God loves when his righteous people intercede for others. However, in the case of prophet Jeremiah, God warned him more than once to not pray for Jerusalem, Judah, and its people. Why did God make this command of Jeremiah? The answer is found in Jeremiah chapters 7, 11, and 14 where God made an indictment against the people by the word of Jeremiah. The people of Judah and Jerusalem were guilty of idolatry, setting up evil altars, disobedience to God's commandments, backsliding, etc. So, because of their wickedness and hard-heartedness, God restrained Jeremiah from praying for them so Yahweh could judge them for their deeds. This judgement came through famine, drought, death by the sword, and destruction.

I had a real-life application of this principle when I desired in my heart to pray for a very well-known celebrity and entertainer. I could see that this particular person was on a hellish trajectory, clearly under great darkness and deception, and was also deceiving others. I was very grieved concerning this celebrity and what they were doing. One day I began to pray for this person asking God to turn their heart and to save them. I thought it was okay to do so, for the Lord himself had instructed me to pray for other celebrities before. However, I didn't even begin to utter a word before the Holy Sprit rose up and said: *"Camille, STOP bemoaning this woman! I will not have you pray for her! She is very wicked and I'm going to curse her and her entire family – watch!"*

To get a picture of how wicked this woman is, the Lord revealed to me that this entertainer was one of the *highest-ranking* witches in the world. Not only was she at the top of the occult ladder, but she was specially commissioned by the enemy to trap people's souls to put them into hell. The Lord revealed blood magic, sex magick, and evil sacrifices were involved. And I knew that he was right.

Celebrities and non-celebrities literally worshipped this entertainer. Her and her family have managed to amass great wealth, influence, and prestige at the high cost of desired spiritual currency – blood. I will not write the name of this person due to potential legal backlash.

I also had the Lord restrain me from praying for another person. This time, I had made conversation with an elderly man at the bus stop I was waiting at downtown. For some reason, he began to tell me about the issues going on in his personal life, and the major one at the time was that his wife was gravely ill in the hospital. I told him that I would pray for him and his wife and then left to my destination when my bus came. Being a woman of my word, I did attempt to pray for the healing of this man's wife. But no matter the attempt, the Holy Spirit instructed me to stop and said that the woman's illness was an *"appointed affliction"* and to leave the matter alone. I, of course, obeyed and that was the end of that.

What I've found is that God is always further maturing, developing, and enhancing our prayer lives. He will show us different strategies of when to pray deliverance prayers, fire/warfare prayers, petition prayers, thanksgiving prayers, etc. In addition, God will also lead us into praying in tongues as well, which of course, is a gift of the Holy Spirit. It is my opinion, based on scripture, that each born-again Christian at some point in their walk will encounter the gift of tongues as they mature in their faith and are filled with the Holy Ghost. Some people encounter it immediately and for others it takes time before the gift manifests. God simply moves differently with different people.

I was filled with the Holy Spirit and led by the Spirit long before God introduced me to the gift of tongues. In fact, it was late one night as I was praying in the understanding when the Lord said to me, "*You are blocking your gift of tongues.*" And when I asked him how that was, God told me to speak what I heard. When I spoke what I heard, another language that I did not understand came out of my mouth. I was so caught up in the logical mechanics of speaking in tongues, that I didn't let the supernatural through my faith takeover. However, when I did, I realized the enemy's attacks waned in several areas. I understood that when I prayed in tongues it stirred up prophecy in me. When I prayed in tongues, I would experience deliverance from demonic spirits. God instructed me to especially pray in tongues before sleeping, which helped with my nighttime warfare. Praying in tongues eventually led to interpretation, which in turn resulted in other gifts being stirred up within me.

Another thing that God began to train me on with prayer, is praying during the night watches. Because I was so sensitive to the spiritual realm in terms of sight and hearing, I would often get spiritually attacked at night. The Lord then shifted me into a program of praying regularly between the hours of 12 AM to 3 AM. I was instructed to pray against witchcraft and demonic attacks during these hours, which also led to me executing self-deliverance at these times as well. I noticed that in my relationship with the Lord that he enjoyed speaking to me at night. It's just me and the Holy Spirit conversing during these precious hours. Almost always he would have me write and record the things he was revealing to me.

Night watch is a season during the night hours when men are usually sleeping, but destinies are challenged, and evil altars are serviced to destroy the sons of men. Therefore, the Lord revealed to me that praying warfare prayers, starting fasts, and receiving prophetic insight and direction during these night hours was highly important for me – especially with my gifting.

Father began training me in several different areas besides the ones mentioned above. As of the writing of this book, I am still in my wilderness season and continue to be trained. I'm still being fortified, still being sharpened. With God, the growth and development of his servants is of utmost importance to him.

In the next few chapters, I'll be talking more about the other areas God has dealt with me in. It really all starts with a sense of knowledge.

8 | THE KNOWING

"But let him that glorieth glory in this, that he understandeth and knoweth me, that I am the Lord which exercise lovingkindness, judgment, and righteousness, in the earth: for in these things I delight, saith the Lord."
Jeremiah 9:24

Currently, we have a generation that champions self and personal contextual truth. They have made a journey of knowing and pursuing self. Self-love. Self-healing. Self-guidance. Self-help. Self-determination. Self-made. Self-taught. His/Her/Their Truth. It's the "me, me, me" society, and how dare you be different enough to think otherwise or have a dissenting opinion. This is the way of the world. The way that tells you, "Live and let live" or to "Live in your truth"; where everything must be validated or else face consequences – whether it be right or wrong.

Do you see the problem? People today are seeking to know and celebrate themselves and their own wisdom without knowing or acknowledging their Creator. In fact, many have put themselves in place of God. If an inventor created the latest patented robot, no one would expect the robot to say that they know themselves apart from the ingenuities of its maker. People don't know God and therefore don't know themselves. That's why most folks hide behind façades and masks.

Today, humans seem to know so much. There's always a new method or trend. They know about CERN, algorithms, politics, science, economics, technology, or history, but they don't appear to know the things that really matter. They don't know the tricks of the enemy, or how God desires to be close to them, or what God's standards are, or what their purpose is in the earth. People just can't seem to get past 'self', the enemy's smoke and mirrors, or the trivialities of life.

As a Chosen One, there are three things that God will intentionally position you to know. You should:

1. Know Thy God (his ways, will, and nature)
2. Know Thyself (your personality, triggers, and purpose)
3. Know Thy Enemy (his devices, intentions, and nature)

Know Thy God
God wants his people to know him in all his various facets. The Bible makes the distinction that the people of Israel knew God's works, but Moses knew God's ways. In this dispensation, God wants us to know him by his Word, his ways, and remembrance of his works. Our Father wants fellowship with us in the same manner he had intimate fellowship with Abraham and Moses. He wants us to connect with him like how Daniel communed with him through prayer. When we know God, we can trust in him and be obedient to him. Many people think they know God. They make blanket statements such as "I'm God's favourite". Yet, the fruit of their lives speaks otherwise. Knowing God is a man's greatest

fulfillment in life. It is a privilege and an honour, and no man can say they know God without being radically and spiritually transformed and changed.

> *"There is no peace like the peace of those whose minds are possessed with full assurance that they have known God, and God has known them, and that this relationship guarantees God's favor to them in life, through death and on for ever."* **- J.I. Packer, Knowing God p. 43**

Know Thyself

Jesus will always reveal the true you. You'd be surprised how many people don't really know themselves. They don't know what their purpose is or what they want out of life. Because they don't have knowledge of self, they seek purpose and identity in things, positions, and other people. When you don't know yourself, you'll allow other people to shape you into their own version of who they think you should be. Who are you really? What is your character like? Where are you going in life? What are your preferences and dislikes? Do *you* know you? The good thing is, God can help you answer these questions. In getting to know God, Jesus will start to tell you about you. He'll address your deficiencies, qualities, and heart. He'll let you know your strengths and lovingly help you through your weaknesses. You'll be shocked at what God can show you about who you are. You have to examine and know yourself as a Chosen One.

> "Let us search and try our ways, and turn again to the Lord." **– Lamentations 3:40**

"Thus saith the Lord of hosts; Consider your ways." – **Haggai 1:7**

"For I say, through the grace given unto me, to every man that is among you, not to think of himself more highly than he ought to think; but to think soberly, according as God hath dealt to every man the measure of faith." – **Romans 12:3**

Know Thy Enemy
Our enemy knows the ways of men better than we humans do. He's spent millennia watching us, learning our weaknesses, taking advantage of us, and destroying some of us. In order to escape the enemy's grasp, we need to know how he operates, the devices he employs, and how he targets us as Believers specifically. The way how Satan attacks you might not be the same way he attacks another brother or sister in Christ. God made us as unique individuals, and therefore Satan has different and specific schemes he likes to use for each person. We need to identify the enemy's patterns in our lives; when he likes to attack, the people he likes to use, and the weapons he chooses to target us with.

"Lest Satan should get an advantage of us: for we are not ignorant of his devices." – **2 Corinthians 2:11**

"Be sober, be vigilant; because your adversary the devil, as a roaring lion, walketh about, seeking whom he may devour." – **1 Peter 5:8**

My Knowing

KNOWING GOD

Knowing God is a life-long mission filled with interesting experiences and lessons along the way. Truly, I started to get to know God from a child and through my tribulation and deliverance. But it has been through my wilderness and training period that I have come to know more about God.

I have known that God is a true Father. I had mentioned in chapter 1 that I had a low self-esteem going back to my childhood. I was overweight and teased about it in school. I also thought I was ugly, even at the start of adulthood. The way how I saw myself as a young lady was skewed by self-hatred, rejection, depression, and anger. But a father's job is to help his daughter see herself through his eyes of love, care, and kindness. It is also a father's job to protect, provide, counsel, cover, and direct. While my earthly father ticked off some of these boxes, Dad being imperfect, did not meet some of these points in his relationship with me.

My Dad was a provider and a hard worker. He was protective of both my mother and me. And while he was not cold, he was emotionally distant, passive, and mostly aloof. While I craved to spend time with my Dad playing chess, cricket, or going out to activities, he was always working. In fact, I grew up in a home in which my Dad always put his job before his family. He seemed to either not see or care that it affected his marriage or his relationship with me. My mother on the other hand was everything a mother should be. She was nurturing, caring, asked the right questions, talked with me, and enjoyed spending time with me. Even as I grew into adulthood, while my mother's relationship with me turned into a friendship, my relationship with my Dad was somewhat distant with my Mom acting as a kind of mediator. Dad simply did not know how to form conversation with me, was stubborn, and sometimes argumentative, so my Mom would update him on what was going on in my life.

However, as I got to know God through the Bible and through the medium of prayer, my eyes were opened to the fathering he was doing in my life. I remember near to the time of my deliverance I went to use the bathroom. And while looking into the mirror, I heard the Holy Spirit in an excited voice tell me, *"You are beautiful!"* For some reason, I needed to hear those words. It's not that I hadn't heard them before – my Mom and Dad would always tell me this. But those words coming from a father's heart mean more when a broken daughter hears them.

Scripture indeed has it right when it states that we are "…fearfully and wonderfully made…" (Psalm 139:14). God started to remind me of this scripture whenever I would speak negatively of myself. He also gave me specific instructions with regards to my eating habits, vitamin intake, and exercise routines. Obeying his instructions resulted in me losing and maintaining a healthy weight.

The Lord would also lovingly encourage me to get my hair done, take some rest when needed, put on a fancy outfit or makeup when going out. These things may seem little to you, but for me at that time, these were big changes and much needed. But hearing the Lord direct me in these things showed me his love for me as a Father, and he nudged me into receiving this love in its purity.

When I was worried about not being able to make a bill payment, suddenly money would come into my bank account. That was Father's provision. When I came near to getting into a car accident, something happened where I suddenly swerved and made it out the way in time. That was Father's providence. When a friendly enemy was jealous and attempted to hurt me, God cut them off from me. That was Father's protection. God is a good Father, and I've come to know this through experiencing the manifestation of his Word. I've lived it.

I've also come to know God as a friend. It is one of the most wonderful things experiencing friendship with God. As I mentioned before, all of the friends I had made at university were no longer my friends, and God told me it would happen before it did. I was then left in a new city with estranged family members and very few meaningful connections. I was lonely and felt very isolated, particularly as all of this happened near to the COVID-19 pandemic occurring. I attempted to make friends at the churches I attended, but nothing ever seemed to stick. I further understood that many church people didn't practice what they preached, which made me angry and not want to interact with too many folks. During this time of refinement and alignment, God revealed himself to be my friend.

The Lord would talk to me about any and everything. Any time I had a question; he would answer it. He would shift my mindset from negativity to biblical truth whenever he noticed certain patterns in my thinking. I remember before leaving Kaycee's house, God told me, "*They* (meaning Kaycee and her family) *won't help you. Neither will your extended relatives. But I will send people and move people to come to your aid. You will be helped by Me. I am your Helper."* A friend helps their friends, and Jehovah Jireh decided he was going to be my friend and help me.

When I tell you that he did exactly what he said he would do! I had complete strangers that didn't look like me, had no vested interest in me, and who didn't even know me assist me when I had to move, helped me with getting jobs, talk with me through depressive episodes, and water me when I was faint. God was a friend to me – just like he was to Abraham. He was the friend that saw me cry myself to sleep many nights. God was the friend that saw my broken heart when I was in pain and walked me through it. He was the friend that gave me resources when I needed it. And the friend that poured out favour on me because he wanted to see me move into higher heights. I knew God because he manifested his Word in my life and through knowing him, I learned his will for my life.

KNOWING MYSELF

Before I came to Christ, I couldn't tell you about myself. I knew things about myself, but I didn't really know who I was. However, having God be a Father and friend to you will fully make you aware of who you are, because he will tell you. I knew I was a smart person, but I never thought anything of it. I simply loved to learn new things and increase my capacity in various areas. However, God highlighted this to me more as I grew in my wilderness season. *"I'm going to use your intelligence,"* Holy Spirit said. I, being me, asked the Lord 'why?'. His response was, *"You are smart. I made you that way for a reason, you know."* Here was the God of the universe telling me that he created me to be smart and that he would use that aspect of me. But my smartness seemed to affect my relationships which I didn't understand initially. It was part of internal personality issues, which God wanted to correct.

In my sessions with Minister Clarence, I also learned something else. My whole life up until then, I always thought I was weird. I was very quiet, serious, and focused at first, but if someone got to know me, they'd tell you how goofy, genuine, and kind I was. I never liked being around large groups of people, neither did I enjoy small talk on trivial matters. I preferred to have meaningful conversations and was very independent (I usually don't depend on people to do much for me, I'm a "get up and go get it" type of person and only ask for help when needed). I always was an *internalist* so to speak, having a dynamic mental landscape of thought, so that I kept myself good company. I was reserved but not shy and very observant of people and my surroundings. My introverted personality more than likely was part of me growing up as an only child.

Then Minister Clarence decided to talk to me about it one day. He asked me if I knew my personality and made me take a personality test. Once I got the results, he explained to me that my personality was created by God, and that I was designed to have certain ways of thinking and interacting that may differ from others. Knowing my personality would assist me with having a better relationship with others (and myself), especially once I got a grasp on my triggers. God showed me that Minister Clarence was right. I had spent nights praying that God would change me and make me more "normal," but he would just end up rebuking me and telling me he would do no such thing. God straight up told me, *"You're not normal and you never will be. Get comfortable with this. You're different and made to be so."*

By getting to know myself through God's eyes and my personality, Father began to reveal to me what my gifts were. I could always write from a young age. This love of writing mostly came from a love of reading which my mother instilled in me. I loved to write poetry, songs, essays – all types of stuff. I found better ways to express myself in writing that I did in speaking. It wasn't that I couldn't speak (I had won speech competitions and debates in school), I just loved writing and could do it fairly well. God showed me that this was a gift and that I also had a scribal anointing on my life.

In addition, I could sing. It was something that I started doing as a teenager. At first, I didn't think I was any good, but in secondary school my friends heard me and told me I sang great. This made me more interested in music. My mother supported me learning to play the guitar after messing around with my uncle's old one, and that made me start to play and sing. When I came to Christ, the Lord encouraged me more and more to write songs of worship and praise and to sing. I noticed that it was something I loved to do, as easy as breathing. But now, when I sang, I felt Holy Spirit show up. Then, I started to sing in tongues which turned into prophetic singing and songs. God was using my natural talents to help develop my spiritual gifts and I simply loved doing it.

As God showed me more about myself, he also had to expose what my triggers were. When I say triggers, I mean the things that cause us to get upset or potentially react negatively. Holy Spirit was aiding me to understand these triggers so I could have better responses when faced with certain situations. One of my triggers was rejection. I experienced many situations as a child and teenager where I was not welcomed in some friendship or social groups. When confronted with these situations, I would either have an outburst, ignore these individuals, or stick to myself. I became a loner because of this, even into my adulthood.

However, God revealed that often I internalized a lot of the meanness and negativity by turning it into anger. In fact, while in primary school, it wasn't uncommon for my teachers to report to my parents that I was an "angry child". What they didn't tell my parents is that I was often bullied about my weight, my appearance, and class status (Barbados is a country that has a classism and elitism social structure). All they saw was the response, but not the antecedent.

I was angry at the way I was treated and angry for being so different than everyone else. When I got saved, two of the first things to go were anger and self-hatred. But rejection extended beyond my childhood and teenage years. It followed me as an adult, especially being a born-again Christian. Now I wasn't different just because of my unique personality, I was also different because I carried the light of Holy Spirit in me. The Lord purposely put me in places and situations where I was rejected by people – even some family members – and then he walked me through how to deal with it in a healthy and godly way. I recognised through these exercises that my go-to and preferred way of dealing with things was to remain quiet. I would rather stay silent than to open my mouth and say things that I couldn't take back. It didn't surprise me then that people began to hate this mode of operation because I didn't react in the way they thought I would. But I knew that doing things this way saved me from being in trouble with the Lord and dealing with people's ignorance.

Furthermore, my wilderness season was tough because I desired to have good and godly friends. The Lord had other plans during my wilderness season and kept me mostly alone. I didn't like it at the time, but I needed to learn myself and learn how to be at peace with who I was and who God called me to be. God exposed and enhanced my character: kind, thoughtful, a giver, a hard-worker, intentional, insightful, and willing to learn and grow. I began to recognise that people who encountered me began to see all of these things too.

I needed to know myself and God assured me that when that process was over to the glory of God, that he would then send the right people into my life as destiny helpers, partners, and kingdom relationships. By going through the wilderness, I began to understand my purpose: to worship Almighty God and to be used by him in ministry to reach his people.

KNOWING THE ENEMY

The enemy loves to re-open old wounds, re-establish broken covenants, and entangle the Believer in past sins. This is our enemy's nature – to destroy us by hook or crook. One day as I was going about my business, I heard the Holy Spirit utter these words, *"The enemy is not your friend."* And it is true. Satan and his cohorts mean us humans harm, and they are not our friends. I learned these things early on as I began to gain my legs in this Christ-walk.

Post-deliverance, I was doing everything I should have been doing, but there were still evident weaknesses I needed to overcome. One of these weaknesses included the area of condemnation. There was something about being a perfectionist as a child that seemed to make me more prone to attack in this area.

Additionally, God brought to my attention the need for me to break generational curses. Demons still had access to me through these open doors and used it against me to attack me with witchcraft and dream pollution. It started first with me going through repentance and renunciation of the curses upon myself and my family because of ancestral participation in freemasonry and witchcraft. I remember going through a very extensive prayer that the Lord walked me through to destroy those curses and altars. By doing this I realised that many spiritual attacks I faced started to dissipate. Through this experience, I learned that repenting is different from renouncing. When we repent, we turn away from the sins of our fathers. But when we renounce, we break the agreement our forefathers had with certain spirits and iniquities, which provides deliverance.

Now, many churches don't speak on the realities of fighting demonic thoughts. This of course was how the demon of perversion through a generational curse would seek to attack me.

I would be randomly going about my business when a sexually perverse thought would enter my mind. I had no interest in such things, but yet these thoughts would come, and when they did – I would rebuke them swiftly in Jesus' name. I knew the thoughts were demonic as I had discerned the source. As I mentioned in chapter one, many relatives on my father's side of the family seemed to be in some sort of sexual sin or dealing with sexual perversion. That was the reality of my spiritual foundation. Even before I got deliverance, the Lord highlighted to me that there was a curse of perversion released upon my family due to my grandmother (my father's mother). The Lord showed me that because this curse was still in place over my life, these sexual demons had access to plant thoughts. I had already closed the spiritual doors I opened due to watching pornography, but I didn't close the door that was from the family curse.

During the earlier periods of my life post-deliverance, I was bombarded with dreams that featured my dead grandmother (my father's mother) trying to talk to me, and in dreams I often found myself in the family home that was formerly owned by my dead grandmother. I would always awake, rebuke, and cancel or nullify the effects of such dreams. However, the dreams kept coming. I knew the dreams were demonic because the Word of God made it clear that, "the dead know nothing" (Ecclesiastes 9:5) and that we were not supposed to be communing with the spirits of the dead. One day after waking up from such a dream, the Holy Spirit pressed upon me to break the generational curse over my life – that was the key to stopping these dreams. You see, the familiar spirit of perversion was attempting to have a covenant with me the same way it had one with my grandmother. Therefore, this same familiar spirit would show up in my dreams wearing the mask of my grandmother's face.

So, I started to pray. I asked God for forgiveness for the sins of my grandmother and all other family members that resulted in the curse of perversion polluting the bloodline. I repented, renounced, and broke the curse of perversion; asking God to purge and purify my bloodline and that of my future lineage. After finishing prayer, I could sense the Holy Spirit being very pleased at what I had done. The proof of this was in the dream that I received the same night I completed these prayers.

In the dream I was in the garden of my dead grandmother's house (she was not around at all). Where I was in the garden allowed me to see a round silver balloon that was tied by a string to a pole standing in the dirt. For some reason in this dream, I was drawn to the balloon and knew that I had to access it and take it with me (I discerned it was some sort of prize/reward in the dream). However, when I attempted to go after the balloon to take it, a gruff voice of a man echoed behind me asking, "what are you doing here?" When I turned around to see who was talking to me, I saw that it was a male family member that was a homosexual in real life addressing me. This male family member then approached to attack me. But in this dream, I had the ability to see and sense what type of punch, jab, and hit this family member would attack me with before he even

did. Therefore, I was able to avoid being hit by him and instead returned an assault of hits and punches which led to this male family member being injured. Seeing that he had lost the fight, the family member looked at me, told me to "go", and then disappeared. I retrieved the balloon from the pole and exited the compound of the family house, and then I saw myself happily walking down the street of the neighbourhood.

The above dream illustrated that I had successfully broken the curse of perversion from over me and loosened the enemy's grip in that area over my life. The male family member in the dream represented the familiar spirit of perversion that had plagued my father's household, including myself. Me fighting this familiar spirit, winning, and retrieving the silver balloon was showing victory in this spiritual battle. After I had the above dream, I didn't have anymore issues of dreaming about dead family members. I learnt that dreaming of dead family members was God allowing the enemy to mask himself as our deceased relatives, highlighting the generational and foundational problems with our bloodlines. Satan likes to use the pollution of bloodlines against God's people.

Father God also exposed the strategy of the enemy to get me to open doors of sin in my life. I had still struggled with condemnation, and so Satan saw this as an entry point to bring oppression, depression, guilt, shame, and fear into my life. One night I was at work and began to pray during my shift. The Holy Spirit began to speak to me – "*You know, the enemy only accesses you when you condemn yourself. He uses that as his opening, his bait.*" I began to understand this reality only too quickly. A few months after the Lord told me this, I had had a rough week. But what I noticed one day was that the Lord was not talking to me. I prayed as I usually do, but Holy Spirit was not responding to me as he normally does. I knew for certain that something was wrong. And so, when I got home, I began to pray, asking the Lord why he wasn't speaking to me. As soon as I asked, I had a vision. I saw an open door with a dwarf-like devilish goblin peeking behind the door at me. Understanding immediately what the vision meant, I then followed up and asked Holy Spirit how I opened a door for the enemy. His response was *"condemnation"*.

I went through such a rough couple of days back then that I started to pummel myself for mess-ups and things gone awry. I didn't even realize my own sin even though I had been battling condemnation like a soldier. I then started to repent, renounce, and break any curses I opened myself to. Afterwards, the Lord said in a very stern tone, *"Camille, you must not condemn yourself. When you do so, it hurts me."*

Well, those simple words pricked my heart, and I knew I had to take this battle seriously. To know that the Lord was hurt concerning my condemnation put everything in perspective for me. I began to see how the enemy would cause situations to arise with people and how I had to temper my reactions to prevent these occurrences of condemnation. I worked out my own salvation with fear and trembling. The Lord had loosed me from the grip of perfectionism, and so I knew I could be loosened from condemnation as well.

What I love about Father is that whenever the enemy would be up to his tricks, he would send me a warning. I remember one time; I was in a tough season with so much going on around me. There was so much distraction and disappointment, but I wasn't responding the way I necessarily should have. Well, God decided to show me something when I went to sleep to get me back into shape. I had a dream:

I was on a bridge that looked similar to the Golden State Bridge. The bridge was over water and people were walking over it and standing and talking. There was a mature looking man beside me, and I noticed him out of the side of my eye. I seemed to have started to take in the scenery, however, out of nowhere I saw two lions appear. The lions darted towards the mature looking gentleman who was standing next to me overlooking the bridge, and they began to maul him and rip him to shreds. For some reason though, the lions never made a move towards me. Blood was everywhere and it was clear the lions were out for the hunt and for the kill.

When I woke up, the Holy Spirit reminded me, *"The enemy prowls around like a roaring lion seeking whom he may devour."* The dream was a warning to be especially careful how I was walking, and to avoid becoming the enemy's prey.

There is power in knowing. Knowing God, yourself, and your enemy positions you as a Chosen One to become a conqueror at every level. What I mentioned above are just some of the examples I have to share about this topic. We don't need worldly, self-centred knowledge, but the knowledge and wisdom that is in alignment with the word of God. From knowledge, however, comes understanding – and as much as we should know God, we also need to understand him and how he operates.

9 | THE UNDERSTANDING

"Wisdom is the principal thing; therefore get wisdom: and with all thy getting get understanding."
Proverbs 4:7

Understanding something (or someone) is the greatest thing there is. Have you ever had a math problem to solve and busted your brain figuring out the right mechanics to apply to obtain the right answer? But, when you understood how PEDMAS works, calculating the answer to the equation became a breeze? It's also like how we understand that to determine the amount of force we need to multiply mass by acceleration. Now, understanding God can't be broken down via mathematics or physics, but to understand God, who he is, and how he operates can be summed up in the following formula:

THE WORD OF GOD + RELATIONSHIP WITH JESUS CHRIST (and the experiences/lessons under the tutelage of the Holy Spirit) = **UNDERSTANDING OF GOD**.

We can't understand Almighty God apart from his Word. We also cannot fully understand who God is without a relationship with him through his Son, Jesus.

"The entrance of thy words giveth light; it giveth understanding unto the simple." — **Proverbs 119:130**

"Now we have received, not the spirit of the world, but the Spirit which is of God; that we might know the things that are freely given to us of God." — **1 Corinthians 2:12**

Understanding God means understanding that He is a multi-faceted Divine Being, who loved his creation so much that he sent Jesus Christ, his Son, to die for the sins of all humanity and has given us redemption through his blood. Most of God's personality and purpose is wrapped up in the fact that he exists in the duality of being both the Lamb of God and the Lion of Judah (both of which manifested in the Word made flesh).

As a Chosen One, it becomes clear that we start to understand specific things about God that enable us to continue in our journey of destiny fulfillment. We come to understand that God:

1. Tests his people.
2. Uses our enemies to bless us and sharpen us.

Testing

God is a God who tests his people. Like a good teacher, God assesses our knowledge and understanding of him by reviewing our application of his Word. There are two outcomes – you either pass, showing your understanding, or fail, indicating a need for re-training, re-application, refinement, and improvement. God is a God that intentionally goes through the trouble of proving if you are what you say you are, and he'll investigate what you are made of. Our Father will not allow us to be elevated to a new level until we pass the tests of the current level we're on. Testing builds character and transforms negative and hindering mindsets into victorious and godly ones. Passing God's tests releases promotion over your life and increases spiritual rank. Job is the perfect example in the Bible of being tested. God allowed Satan to have access to torment and oppress Job on every side. But after withstanding all the enemy had thrown at him and yielding to God's correction, Job was promoted to a new level where he prospered even more than he did before, and everything he lost was restored.

> "But he knows where I am going. And when he tests me, I will come out as pure as gold." – **Job 23:10**

> "The refining pot is for silver and the furnace for gold, But the Lord tests hearts." – **Proverbs 17:3**

> "The Lord tests the righteous and the wicked; His soul hates the lover of violence." – **Psalms 11:5**

Using Enemies to Our Benefit

When a Christian has a person who is out to destroy them and actively work against them, often it's due to demonic influences and pride/jealousy. These types of people are referred to as enemies (because they are certainly not a friend or ally). God uses a righteous man's enemies to propel him into destiny and build godly character. It happened to David. King Saul was incensed against David since the latter was anointed and prophesied to be the next king, but Saul had the Lord's anointing removed from him. There was also a jealousy that arose in Saul due to the people's admiration of David's valiant skill in battle. All of this caused Saul to have a hatred toward David that even inspired attempts to kill the to-be king. However, God used David's trials with Saul to build David in prayer, worship, war, strategy, mercy, and leadership. The very person that was persecuting David was the one God used to help prepare him for his destiny as the King of Israel. You can read more about this in 1 & 2 Samuel. For some of us, our enemies are our own family members, neighbours, and even "friends."

> "Thou preparest a table before me in the presence of mine enemies: Thou anointest my head with oil; my cup runneth over." – **Psalm 23:5**

> "When a man's ways please the Lord, he maketh even his enemies to be at peace with him." – **Proverbs 16:7**

My Understanding

After leaving Kaycee's house, I moved into my first apartment on my own. The tip on this rental unit came from a friend that I had met at work. At first, my new landlady was very kind, respectful, and considerate. But things quickly changed due to several issues. This landlady refused to do anything legitimately, she accused me wrongfully, she smoked constantly which filtered into my space and affected me, and she entered my apartment repeatedly without me being present or aware. All of this was rather interesting because the Lord had warned me that a season of spiritual warfare would soon manifest in my life. And this word came to pass with the landlord drama.

What was so frustrating is that I received direction from the Lord to move into this apartment in the first place. The situation got so bad that I would have to record conversations with my landlord and screenshot text messages sent to me. I was also prepared to seek legal counsel about the matter. The demons were manifesting in my landlord so much that I would be in my apartment and overhear this woman releasing curses over me. She would even go so far as to pretend to sell her property to intimidate me into leaving. I wondered how much I was expected to take.

During this period, I would pray diligently for God to not only move me from this place, but also that justice would be given for what was being done to me. One night I was praying the Psalms about the situation, and as I closed the prayer, I saw the angel of the Lord dart from out of my bedroom headed on assignment. When I saw the angel go on his mission, I knew that my prayers would be answered. And I was right. [I mentioned some of this in

The Training chapter].

About 4 weeks later a better apartment was on the market and I got confirmation that I could rent at that new building. I packed my belongings and called a moving company without informing my landlord and moved out the same day I told her I would be leaving. She of course was angry, but quite frankly, I didn't care. When I pulled out from that place, I heard the Holy Spirit say, "*You've passed the test.*" I managed to leave that situation without any evil heart toward my former landlord and I handled the situation based on the Word of God. For this reason, God informed me that I had passed the test he had set up for me. The lesson? How to navigate certain aspects of spiritual warfare and understanding that it's not the person but the spirit(s) operating in them. Since this season, I've had many other tests and most of them came in the form of spiritual warfare and various situations I'll discuss later in the book.

God tends to use the people closest to us in our lives via proximity to test us. And, when he is training us, he will give us one test after another that we'll have to pass. Think of Biblical figures like Joseph, David, and Abraham. God tests our hearts, our faith, and our ways. I learned this from my second major test. It involved a neighbour at my new apartment building. A neighbour who was an enemy to me.

It should be noted that at the apartment building I moved to where I encountered this neighbour, I was one of only three people living there who didn't do drugs, had mental issues, or was involved in illegal activity. I often wondered why God even allowed me to move into this type of environment. There was demonic influence over the people living in the building, and it seemed that my presence disturbed the order. This fact became clear from some of the weird experiences I started to have.

Here's one such experience. When I first moved in, I began to play worship and praise music and pray often in the apartment. I noticed that there was some demonic opposition to me engaging in these activities. I would also play worship music on my laptop while taking breaks from working at home. In one particular instance, while taking some downtime, I decided to enjoy some worship music. But when I pressed 'play' the application would not work even after restarting my device multiple times. I thought this was strange as only earlier in the day, my laptop and the application were working fine.

Immediately, I discerned that this was something spiritual. And for some reason I instinctively prayed, "Father, in the name of Jesus, I bind up the spirit interrupting the use of my laptop, and I loose the fire and judgement of God upon it and command it to go!"

What happened next was intriguing, but God opened my spiritual ears, and I began to hear what was happening in the spirit. It seemed that an angel of God had appeared to deal with this spirit, and I heard the demon cry, "What?! Noooo! Murderrrrrrrr!!" God then instructed me to restart the laptop and play my worship music. And guess what? Everything started working as normal, with zero interference. Someone and something did not enjoy me shifting the atmosphere in the building. I would have to regularly anoint my home and pray just to keep my sanity, but I started to see improvement as I passed the tests of spiritual warfare on the home front.

In my first encounter with this neighbour (who lived in the same apartment building), I noticed that they wore an upside-down cross chain (an occult symbol) around their neck. My discernment was sending off alarm bells that this person was highly demonized, which was later confirmed. I couldn't help but hear from other neighbours and community members of this person's illegal escapades (they were well-known to law enforcement). I couldn't help but notice that this person used drugs heavily. Or that he was in a toxic and abusive relationship with his mentally ill girlfriend. And while I was busy minding my business, the enemy was stirring this neighbour up to be a menace. Here was the test from the Lord.

Let's call this neighbour Mike. Mike decided it was a good idea to steal a package that was delivered to me. As I was working from home, I heard the delivery person leave the package at my door. I got up to get my package but also heard a scuffling outside and a loud noise. When I went outside my door the package was gone, even though the company sent me a notification and picture confirmation of its delivery. I knocked on Mike's door, but of course he didn't answer, and of course he was home too (he didn't have a job). I was furious. Luckily, what was taken was not expensive in value.

I went to bed that night and I couldn't sleep. The reason? Mike was blaring his music throughout the entire building with his loudspeaker system and my apartment was closest to his. I could feel the bass reverberating in my chest as I laid on my bed. I tossed and turned, and finally I asked the Lord why this was happening. Holy Spirit said, *"Forgive him."* At that very moment I could feel internally in my heart a tough, coarse, seed-like element that was wedged into it. It was the seed of unforgiveness. I quickly repented, renounced, and forgave. The moment I finished; the music immediately stopped. What didn't stop was the intimidation and targeting that Mike was doing to me. In fact, because I filed a noise complaint due to Mike's excessively loud music, it triggered a 2-year battle of incessant harassment on his end.

Everything came to a head when Mike started tampering with my door and property. He destroyed my peephole and started putting tape and glue all over my apartment entrance. The landlord knew about this situation but was rather powerless to do anything. The police knew about it but couldn't seem to do anything. I had had enough. One day as the torment continued, I became so frustrated that I cried out to the Lord in anger. I prayed, "Lord, if I had the opportunity, I would strangle this man without feeling a thing!" I was burning with rage. But God's response was simple – *"Pray for him. I see everything he's doing to you. Just pray for him. The enemy is using him."* I did just that. It was a hard thing to do, but I was reminded that in God's word we're to bless those who curse us and pray for those who abuse us (Luke 6:28).

However, the Lord knew my boldness and personality so well that just in time, he made a way for me to move into a better, quieter, and more comfortable apartment. In fact, the Lord used the situation with Mike to propel me further into destiny.

MY UNDERSTANDING

By moving to a new place due to the situation, a complete transition happened in my life. I found a prophetic and apostolic church and Christian community I didn't even know existed in my city. I met with elders, intercessors, evangelists, prophets, and kingdom organizers. God led me to this new kingdom community to mature me, sharpen me, and surround me with people who lovingly kept me accountable, nurtured my gifts, and poured into me. In this way I started to further strengthen my gifts and had confirmation of my calling. It was all a set-up. An enemy turned out to be a used pawn. If I had stayed at that apartment and in that part of my city, I would not have encountered the places to help me grow as God wanted me to. Passing the test led to transition and elevation.

Today, as I live, Mike is dead. He was found 2 years later in the same apartment he had with only his dog watching over his body. I do not rejoice at his departure, because he did not live right. I wish he had known Jesus Christ before he died, but from what I've heard, he continued to live the same sinful life. It was strange how everything unfolded. It is strange how God deals with people who rise up against his children. Stranger still is the way how God will put his children into tough situations to prove them. It certainly is strange, but when we understand God's methods, it begins to make sense.

By passing the tests, God changed my name and shifted me to where I needed to be.

10 | THE NAMING

"And the Gentiles shall see thy righteousness, and all kings thy glory: and thou shalt be called by a new name, which the mouth of the LORD shall name."
Isaiah 62:2

Everything in the earth, seas, and heavens has a name. A person, place, or thing (nouns) will always be referred to by a name. Elements, entities, and beings in the spiritual realm all have names attached to them (Mark 5:8-10). What most ancient humans understood was that names carried power and to name a thing came from immense authority. In fact, this authority of naming was given to Adam (the first man) in the Book of Genesis. The ancient peoples also knew that to be named after one's god made a person wield the force or potency of that god. For this reason, many from the nation of Israel had names that contained El, Yahu, or Yah for they were named by inspiration and in proximity to Yahweh (the God who delivered them from Egypt).

Today, names are given to newborns based on whether or not the parents like the sound or trend of a name. Celebrities have named their children everything from 'Apple' to 'North.' The names have no deep or solid meaning (with probably little effort of thought) but are just based on things or preferences.

In some Nigerian tribes (much like Jewish people), names are a really big deal. Naming a child is such a momentous event that a naming ceremony is held within a week of the child's birth, and the parents make known the newborn's name. For members of the Yoruba or Igbo tribes, having Oluwa or Chukwu/Chi as part of the name indicates the name's reference to God, and often carries a prophetic meaning that the child will grow up to manifest. For this reason, naming a child in these cultures is an act of prophesying over the new baby – as is seen in scripture.

Here are some examples:

Oluwadamilola (Yoruba name) – God has brought me wealth.
Oluwaseun (Yoruba name) – Gift of God or God, thank you.
Oluwatoyin (Yoruba name) – God is worthy of praise.
Chidiebere (Igbo name) – God is merciful.
Chimamanda (Igbo name) – My God will not fall or fail me.
Chukwudumaga (Igbo name) – God, lead me.

Likewise, many names of places and people in the Bible were and are prophetic in nature. Andrew Hopkins of Breaker Ministries had this to say on the subject:

> *"Names are powerful. Culture has shifted over time and Westerners don't seem to have as much depth and value for the potential in a name...Biblical Israel had a rich value for names...and ultimately it was reflective of God,*

who hides prophetic potential, identity, and function in a name." – **A. Hopkins, (2019), The prophetic potential hidden in a name | www.breakerministries.com**

All throughout the scriptures, people fulfilled the prophecies of their names. The name, Jacob means "supplanter" and he did indeed supplant his brother Esau for the firstborn inheritance (Genesis 27:36). In 1st Samuel chapter 25, we read about Nabal's mistreatment of David and his men. Due to the unfair treatment, David was ready to destroy Nabal's house by the sword. However, Nabal's wife Abigail was able to wisely intervene by placating David, reminding the king-to-be that her husband's name meant "fool", and Nabal was embodying the name by acting foolishly toward David (verse 25). Jesus' birth was prophesied by angel Gabriel to Mary in Luke chapter 1, and the name Jesus (Yeshua) means "to deliver or to rescue". Jesus fulfilled the prophecy concerning his name by dying on the cross for the sins of mankind to save man from death through redemption in his shed blood.

Even more interesting concerning names in the Bible was that God often changed the names of people in both the Old and New Testaments. Jacob was changed to Israel (meaning "God preserves" or "he wrestles with God") after wrestling with the angel of God (Genesis 32:25-31). Abram ("high father") was changed to Abraham (meaning "father of many nations") and Sarai ("my princess") to Sarah (meaning "princess of multitudes") in Genesis 17:5,15. In Jesus' time (Matthew 16:16-18), he changed Simon ("he who hears") to Peter ("rock"). Jesus also surnamed two of his disciples

James and John the sons of Zebedee with Boanerges, meaning "Sons of Thunder" (Mark 3:17). In certain circumstances, God gave people their names by informing their parents before their birth as we see in the case of John the Baptist (Luke 1:13).

God himself is also known by many names, as each name manifests a different facet or aspect of God's character and purpose. Yahweh Jireh will provide for his people. Yahweh Rapha will heal his people. Yahweh Tsidkenu is the righteousness of his people. Yahweh M'Kaddesh will sanctify his people. The I AM is the name that Israel first knew God by. Jesus' disciples called him Rabbi and Adonai. The Holy Spirit is referred to as the Spirit of Truth or the Spirit of God. God is a God who prioritizes names. The Bible states that all of us will receive new names in heaven and that God will give us a new name by which we can refer to him as well (Revelations 2:17 and 3:1).

Today, in this dispensation, God is still giving people names that hold prophetic value and inheritance. While many don't discuss it in churches, it doesn't mean that it isn't happening. Chosen ones have a name that God calls them by and considers it a part of their identity. Knowing our identity in Christ can also be proved by our name.

My Naming

MY NAMING

As I mentioned in chapter 1, my parents named me Camille. I was given this name by inspiration of my father's name. Growing up, my mother would tell me that my name meant "beautiful". However, I don't think either of my parents understood the meaning of my name.

Additionally, I was given the middle name Christina after my great-grandmother who left a positive impression on my mother while she was alive. My great-grandmother (on my father's side) was said to be a sweet and kind woman who had high-brown skin and a peaceful demeanour. My parents always remarked that phenotypically I received my skin complexion from her. When I became a young adult and was searching for meaning and purpose, God directed me to study and understand my name.

Camille is a derivative of *Camilla* which comes from the Latin *Camillus*. It is a unisex name which can be either masculine or feminine. Although it has its origins in Latin, it also has strong French roots and is translated as "helper to the priest", or "acolyte", or "free-born servant", or "virginal". Some Latin interpretations and derivations point to the name also meaning "noble" or "honourable". In Roman mythology, my name is based on an Amazon warrior and huntress named Camilla who was a daughter of the goddess Diana.

The name **Christina** is obvious in its meaning. It is the female derivative of Christian, meaning "a follower of Christ", which also has Latin origins. It comes from the word *Christianus* which comes from the Greek word *khristós*.

Without really knowing it, my parents named me something

very special. Altogether, God has given me this meaning:

Camille Christina = a helper to the priest who serves at the altar of her God and is a follower of Jesus Christ.

By accepting Jesus into my life, I walked right into the prophetic embodiment of my name at birth. And, by deciding to grow in the Spirit and in the things of God, I started walking in the destiny and prophecy of my name.

But my naming didn't just stop with my parents. I've been called "Cam" or "Cami" by the people around me all my life. Then upon encountering Jesus, God decided to give me two new names so far on my chosen journey with Him.

When I was enduring my tribulation and warfare in my university's city, I received my first name. As I was battling the spiritual chaos that was ensuing around me, the Holy Spirit said to me, "*It's time for you to be used* **Ishayahu**." At first, I was very confused. Why was God referring to me this name? However, God kept calling me *Ishayahu* over and over in my prayer time, to the point where one day I asked why he was calling me this name. At the time, while still completing my university studies, I was also doing Bible study and research into Hebrew and Aramaic. So, the Holy Spirit impressed on me to breakdown the name and study it.

Isha = Woman (in Hebrew)

Yahu = G-d or a short term for Yahweh (in Hebrew, a suffix)

Isha•Yahu = Woman of God

What is so interesting is that since post-deliverance, people that I didn't even know that well started to call me "Woman of God". They could see the anointing on my life and the gift I carried. Each time someone referred to me as such, I would inwardly cringe. The reason why? I didn't really consider myself to be a "Woman of God". All I knew was that I loved Jesus and wanted to live for him. I don't like titles. To me, titles are like compliments...they make me feel uncomfortable and awkward. But, when I communed with the Holy Spirit in prayer, he would remind me that the reason people were referring to me as a "Woman of God" was because it was my *name* (a name that I was embodying – supernaturally).

About two years post-deliverance, I was in my new city and the Lord revealed the second name he had for me. It was at the start of the COVID-19 pandemic and lockdown season. I had taken to praying and fasting during this time. One day I was praying and meditating when Holy Spirit impressed on me, *"You are Gedaliah!"* I could literally feel the Holy Spirit smiling on me in joy. I asked him what that meant, and his response was to look up the Hebrew. So, I did.

Gedaliah = גדליה = Made Great by God

God was naming me Gedaliah as a prophetic inference of the great things he would use me to do. He confirmed this to me through another prophetic word by a fellow sister in Christ who said that I would be a history-maker, and that God would use me to shift things in the nation of Canada.

Altogether, God named me exactly who I am and continue to grow into. The two names are very prophetic.

Ishayahu Gedaliah = A Woman of God who is made great by God.

The Lord has been before me, behind me, beside me, above me, and all around me. His presence in my life makes me great. It is his hand that has guided me into destiny and victory. I have learned to embrace these two names. They are who I am until he calls me home.

Along my journey, I've encountered other Christians who either had their names changed by God or were given new names by him. Often, it was because their former names were associated with pagan deities or had occult meanings, or God also just wanted to prophesy a new thing over them.

Names hold a promise for tomorrow. It was through naming me (as God has named other saints) that God revealed his promises to me. Promises which I hold dear. Promises which I've had to fight for.

11 | THE PROMISE

"Let us hold fast the profession of our faith without wavering; (for he is faithful that promised)."
Hebrews 10:23

God's promises concerning his people are always connected to destiny. All throughout the scriptures, God promised inheritances, generations, promotions, prosperity, and positions to his people. What's fascinating is that most of the promises God made to his people weren't just for them, but for those who would come after them. God's promises stand forever.

In the Bible, God promises to be with us and never leave us. He promises to love and protect us. Our Lord promised to supply our needs, to direct our paths, to guide our way, to forgive us when we sin, and on and on. He promised us eternal life through Jesus Christ. God has made a myriad of promises to his people, and he is faithful through Christ Jesus to perform what he has promised to us.

> "For all the promises of God in him are yea, and in him Amen, unto the glory of God by us." **– 2 Corinthians**

1:20

"Know therefore that the LORD thy God, he is God, the faithful God, which keepeth covenant and mercy with them that love him and keep his commandments to a thousand generations." – **Deuteronomy 7:9**

Here's the thing. Sometimes when God promises something to us, we grow impatient when we don't see its immediate manifestation. We don't understand that the promise sometimes includes waiting. This was the case for Sarah and Abraham. The Lord promised that Abraham would be a father of many nations and would have a son from his own loins. Sarah laughed at this promise since she was barren and old. She grew impatient and convinced her husband to procreate with Hagar, her servant. But Ishmael was not the promised son. And, after Hagar gave birth to Ishmael, she began to mock Sarah which caused confusion in Abraham's house, resulting in Hagar being sent away (see Genesis chapters 16-21).

When we don't fully trust and believe God to fulfill his promise to us, we can make decisions that he never intended us to make with results that do not promote the success of promise. It turns out that Sarah eventually found faith in God's promise, which allowed her to then give birth to Isaac as we see in the Book of Hebrews.

> "Therefore Sarah laughed within herself, saying, After I am waxed old shall I have pleasure, my lord being old also? And the Lord said unto Abraham, Wherefore did Sarah laugh, saying, Shall I of a surety bear a child, which am old? Is any thing too hard for the Lord? At the time appointed I will return unto thee, according to the

time of life, and Sarah shall have a son." – **Genesis 18:12-14**

"For it is written, that Abraham had two sons, the one by a bondmaid, the other by a freewoman. But he who was of the bondwoman was born after the flesh; but he of the freewoman was by promise." – **Galatians 4:22-23**

"Through faith also Sara herself received strength to conceive seed, and was delivered of a child when she was past age, because she judged him faithful who had promised. Therefore sprang there even of one, and him as good as dead, so many as the stars of the sky in multitude, and as the sand which is by the sea shore innumerable." – **Hebrews 11:11-12**

It takes faith to receive and revel in the promises of God. It takes trusting God's way even when we can't see the full vision; knowing that he's faithful to bring everything he said to pass. So many people have been promised things by mere men and have found very few to be trustworthy. Yet God is a faithful and enduring God. We can have full faith and trust in him.

"Most men will proclaim every one his own goodness: but a faithful man who can find?" – **Proverbs 20:6**

"God is faithful, by whom ye were called unto the fellowship of his Son Jesus Christ our Lord." – **1 Corinthians 1:9**

In the chapter 9, I mentioned how God tests his people. A major test that a Chosen One will have to pass is the test of faith concerning what has been promised. Abraham passed this same test when God instructed him to offer up Isaac as a sacrifice, and he obeyed, saying "God will provide a lamb for a burnt offering." And we all know how that story ends. God did in fact provide the sacrifice. A promise from God is an assurance of its manifestation as we abide in him and obey him.

My Promise

MY PROMISE

There have been many promises God has made to me. For obvious reasons, I will not put many of them in this book. When you start walking with God, the promises he makes to you become a very sacred thing. These promises need to be prayed about, meditated on, and cherished as we see the Father bring them to pass.

If you're like me, in addition to the promises in the Bible, you've also had God make promises to you prophetically. This can be through dreams, visions, hearing in the spirit, or prophetic words released over you or through you.

One promise God gave to me that I can mention here, ironically, is connected to the very book you are reading. As you have read these words written by my hand, you've been reading the text that was birthed by a promise from God.

In 2020 during the height of the COVID-19 pandemic, the Lord started talking to me about writing. Coincidentally, my mother became adamant that my testimony was a powerful one that people could read about and gain insight into spiritual things from a Christian perspective. She kept telling me, "You should write a book."

The Lord also began to echo my mother's sentiments when he told me, *"You need to start writing more. Write songs, sermon outlines, stories, poems, and articles. You will write for me."* Truly, many of the things I experienced in coming to Christ and growing in God could be used to teach others. Although the Lord was pushing me to write the book, I had no clue where to start. My heart and emotions were a complete mess over some of the hard things I've had to endure to grow in my calling.

MY PROMISE

I mentioned in The Knowledge chapter that I loved writing since I was a child. Writing was a gift that God had given to me. And, as much as I was apprehensive about writing a book about my testimony, eventually I started. I mostly did this out of frustration.

I HATED sharing with people about my testimony via speaking. I would get called upon to share my testimony and be absolutely aggravated. Not because I didn't want people to know about my "come to Jesus" moment or share in a way to encourage someone to give their life to Christ. But I would be asked to share my testimony in 5-10 minutes, and in my mind – that wasn't enough time. There are so many moving parts to my testimony (some which I haven't been permitted to share in this book) that 5-10 minutes was ridiculous. So, I figured, why not write it? If I wrote it, I wouldn't be asked to verbally explain it.

The structure for the book came to me in a strange way. You see, I like structure. It provides me with a foundation to work with and refer to. God knows this about me, and so one day I was cleaning in my apartment when some of the chapter titles came before me. I thought, this whole ordeal in Christ has been a long story…of a *journey*. I've been on a journey with God, and so many people I've met are on this journey too. Some have even fell off the path. So, people need to know the story about the journey I've been on to live in the calling of God.

And so, I began. I started writing at work, at school, during vacation, at church – wherever I could. I would do research, read the scriptures, and consult with Holy Spirit. Not only did I start writing this book, but Holy Spirit inspired me to start writing other songs, poems, scripts, articles, and manuscripts. Writing became an outlet for me, a way for me to convey things that the Lord had put on my mind and heart.

I remember praying one day and the Lord started speaking so strongly to me about writing. Again, he said, *"You will write for me. Not just the book about your testimony, but other books too. Your books will be known around the world and touch many lives, inspiring and teaching people to live for me. Writing will open the doors of breakthrough in your life. You must write!"*

The Lord was so passionate about this matter. He promised me that certain things would occur because of my obedience to write.

- **Promise #1:** My books will be known around the world.
- **Promise #2:** People will buy my books, and their lives will be touched.
- **Promise #3:** My books will inspire and teach people about God.
- **Promise #4:** Doors of breakthrough (regarding life and ministry) will open (leading to greater things untold).

These are some hefty promises. But I knew it was God because I had a man and a woman of God (who are both legitimate prophets), prophesy similar things to me.

Please know, that if you have bought, were lent, or are reading this book – you are a part of the living manifestation of God's promises to me. And because the Bible says our God lies not, I know these things to be true.

In addition, I would start writing Christian thoughts on my

Facebook page at the time. I would write about things I was seeing in the spirit. Unpopular things. This resulted in people having much to say about me. I'm sure they wondered, *who does she think she is?* My frustration with the platform and with the short articles I wrote being ridiculed caused me to move away from posting. Even though what I posted was true, well-written, and to-the-point, people hated the message of the truth. I began to wonder about God's promises to me. I thought, Lord, they don't even like what I'm writing now – why would you make me write more?

It was then that I noticed how writing has such an acute impact on people. Writing can be used to provoke people to action, to change, to anger, or to obsession. Unfortunately, we also live in a society full of people with shortened attention spans. They want information quickly, and preferably, nothing that would rattle their moral or spiritual compass. I came to understand what the Lord meant when he said, *"You will write for me."* Writing is a weapon. It was Moses' weapon. It was Paul's weapon. It was also David's, Solomon's, and Asaph's weapon. Through this realization, I became encouraged in God's promises to me.

As I reflected on these things, the Lord also reminded me of a prophetic word (a promise) he had given to me related to my books. God had relayed that I would eventually start a book publishing company. While there are fantastic Christian publication companies in existence, I noticed that they mainly published books by ministers or authors with well-known ministries or followings. I was none of these. Most Christian writers today also independently self-publish their work through various online platforms. However, the Lord downloaded a vision for me that was bigger than this. His vision for me included being a front runner in media (written, digital, and visual) and creative industries in the body of Christ.

The Lord's promise to me was clear. Not only would I write for him, but I would also become an agent of creativity to edify the body of Christ via business, the arts, and media. Although Holy Spirit was reminding me of this every chance he got, it sometimes became hard for me to understand. I was just a simple young woman seeking to live the best life possible. I was just a nobody trying to tell everybody about a very special somebody who could save and redeem anybody. I never thought of myself as a pioneer or world-changer. This thought led to the Lord shifting my mindset about who I was and what I had to offer not only to the Church but also to the world.

One day as I was in a contemplative mood, the Holy Spirit said to me, "*Look at your hands.*" When I looked at the palms of my hands, I heard the Lord say, "*These hands will build. You are a Kingdom builder.*" Upon hearing these words, I was left with a faithful assurance about the great things that would take place in the coming years. God said that I would build for him in his Kingdom, and that promise alone connected all the other promises that he so faithfully relayed to me over the years.

Additionally, the Lord promised that I would eventually have a ministry of my own. Again, he highlighted to me that the writing of this book would be the start of part of my ministry. The other aspects of my ministry would include singing and music, deliverance, healing, teaching, preaching, and prophetic demonstration. I honestly found it hard to come to terms with some of these promises since I didn't view myself as any kind of minister. I still had so many things that I thought needed to be sharpened within myself. But lovingly as he usually does, God began to shift my thinking, reminding me that I had already ministered to many people without even realizing it. I was used to praying for people, talked to people about Jesus and the things of God, was on the worship team, did outreach, and many other things. My entire life had already started to be a ministry; I was a living epistle. God just needed to reveal certain things to me and guide me in the way I needed to go.

I had to learn that pursuing and living in the promises of God required fighting. God's promises could not be accessed without overcoming opposition.

12 | THE OPPOSITION

"Blessed be the LORD my strength, which teacheth my hands to war, and my fingers to fight."
Psalm 144:1

Whatever God has promised to his people, Satan will try his best to oppose. Spiritual opposition is something that God's chosen people will have to endure and learn how to fight. Satan and his demonic kingdom network act to directly challenge and disrupt the move and plans of God in the lives of Believers. It is of utmost importance then that the Lord's people learn how to navigate opposition.

Satan does not provide a Believer with opposition unless that chosen vessel is a threat. David was a threat to Saul's political influence and kingship, and so, Saul opposed and persecuted David. Prophet Micaiah was a threat to King Ahab's authority, and so, he was opposed by the king and thrown into prison. John the Baptist was a threat to King Herod, and in the end was beheaded. The apostles were a threat to Roman society's spiritual and political infrastructure, and they were in turn oppressed, imprisoned, and martyred for the gospel's cause. Where the devil is not threatened it will be business as usual. But, when chosen serpent-head-crushers come forth, there is utter mayhem. Why? Born-again Christians carry the power, authority, and presence of the Holy Spirit, and wherever they go, demonic powers will become aware and attempt to oppose. Some see opposition as a bad thing, but in experiencing it we have the capacity to learn, grow, and expand. In the Kingdom of God, it is power *vs* power and altar *vs* altar. As a chosen one, you must engage in the art of spiritual warfare by taking dominion and fighting the good fight.

To handle the spiritual opposition that comes from being a chosen one, there are a few things you need to do:

1. You must look at everything through spiritual eyes (life is very spiritual).
2. You must learn that Satan uses people as his own chosen vessels to oppose you.
3. You must learn that emotions or feelings don't solve spiritual problems, strategic responses and actions do.
4. You must learn the power of holiness as a means of spiritual protection.
5. You must learn to trust and obey God unwaveringly in the face of hellish resistance.
6. You must learn to not fear the enemy but look to God for ways to defeat the enemy.
7. You must learn that opposition is also one of the ways in which God tests and proves his servants. Endeavour to pass these tests for the greater glory.
8. You must understand that opposition is also a

confirmation of God's call upon your life.

"He that dwelleth in the secret place of the most High shall abide under the shadow of the Almighty. I will say of the Lord, He is my refuge and my fortress: my God; in him will I trust. Surely he shall deliver thee from the snare of the fowler, and from the noisome pestilence." – **Psalm 91:1-3**

"No weapon that is formed against thee shall prosper; and every tongue that shall rise against thee in judgment thou shalt condemn. This is the heritage of the servants of the Lord, and their righteousness is of me, saith the Lord." – **Isaiah 54:17**

God shows his chosen soldiers how to navigate spiritual opposition. He provides unique strategies to conquer and defeat an enemy that is continually evolving his malicious methods to ensnare humanity. For the chosen, there are various ways in which Satan and his cohorts will oppose us.

The enemy will oppose us spiritually through:

- Witchcraft attacks (via initiated witches, blind witches, and demons).
- Demonized individuals (persons who are open to demonic suggestion, influence, and transference).
- Releasing confusion, fear, anxiety, doubt, frustration, delay, and disappointment.
- Enticing us to sin against ourselves and others (breaking down our hedge of protection).
- Dream realm attacks or dream pollution.
- Using principalities in our regions to target us and hinder our prayers.

- Creating an atmosphere of weariness or spiritual fatigue in our lives.

There are some critical weapons/tools available to Believers facing spiritual opposition that should never be forgotten:
- The Word of God (our spiritual Sword)
- The fire of God
- The Blood of Jesus
- The Judgement of God
- Binding/loosing
- Destroying evil altars

We can (via God-given authority) loose the fire and judgement of God upon evil spirits that are sent to afflict and attack us. Chosen ones can bind demonic spirits and the machinations of the enemy, and then loose God's plans in the earth. Through the authority in Christ Jesus, we can destroy evil altars erected to divert and oppose our destinies, ministries, families, and churches. Christians can employ the Blood of Jesus to douse the spiritual fire of the enemy.

My Opposition

MY OPPOSITION

Throughout this book so far, I have written about some of the opposition I received when I first gave my life to Christ that led to my deliverance. However, that was only the beginning. Spiritual opposition is something the Christian will continue to encounter throughout their walk with Jesus, and it was exactly so in my case. Before I explain some of the opposition I've experienced, I'd like to talk about why I would have encountered spiritual resistance in the first place.

I've mentioned in a previous chapter that I'm called by God to be a seer. This is a prophetic calling from the Lord that he placed upon my life. I both hear and see from God in unique ways about a myriad of things. In addition to this, I also have an anointing for intercession. I've been called by God to pray and stand in the gap for his people (much like Moses and Daniel were intercessors for Israel). Furthermore, I have a creative anointing upon my life – to make and build things in the creative realm for the Lord and his Church (think of Bezalel [artisan] and David [psalmist]). And I also carry the breaker anointing for breakthrough. Now, I am not mentioning these things in the spirit of pride; I am simply mentioning them because it provides context for the opposition I've experienced. I don't need to prove a point because God can reveal things to people in his own time (I've seen it happen).

Someone like me who is gifted by God in this manner will not be left alone by the forces of darkness. Instead, such a person will become a target for attacks. Witches and warlocks will rise up. Principalities and powers will arise. Demons of every kind will be on the hunt to strategically veer a chosen one like myself from the path of life and righteousness onto a path of destruction and death. My gifting and gifts are not for myself, but God gave them to me to serve others and pull lost sheep out of the fire into the Shepherd's fold. That is why the enemy attacks so hard. Because if I succeed and walk into the fullness of my calling, I am a direct threat to his kingdom and acquisition of souls.

WITCHES AND WITCHCRAFT

By all rights, I should be dead. Of course, the enemy tried to kill me during my tribulation and warfare but failed. However, even afterwards, death was still sent my way. In fact, I had witches congregate to send arrows of death against me. I knew about these arrows by way of prayer and through the dreams the Lord showed me. I'll share one such dream here (I had this dream during a particularly tough and draining season of opposition and spiritual warfare).

I was at a church (being held in a university auditorium) during Sunday service. As the service ended, I started talking with a single mother who was worried about the behaviour of her young son whose father was not involved in his life. The mother had sent her son to speak with the pastor while she was explaining the situation to me. I offered the mother encouragement and told her the Lord would help her. The dream shifted and I was now one of the few people left in the church getting ready to leave. As I turned to go, I saw a young lady who appeared to be a teenager wearing a white t-shirt sitting with two young men. At the back of her shirt, I saw there was the Baphomet symbol in black print. As I looked at it, I discerned that this young lady was a witch. The young woman began to speak to me in the dream and as she spoke, I again discerned that this was a witch addressing

me. The young woman started speaking curses of destruction against me. In the dream, I boldly declared, "Lord, everything that she has used her mouth to utter against me, let it be done to her instead." When I spoke these words, the dream shifted. I was now riding in the backseat of a purple-coloured car traveling along a dark road with the same witch from the church driving wildly in the driver's seat, and the two young men she was with were in the vehicle too. Suddenly, the car became warped and wrapped around and away from me (it was like something from the Matrix movies), and I was now standing on the side of the street watching as the car entered a horrible collision with another white vehicle and imploded in fire. I was unscathed and untouched, but the witch and her accomplices died in the wreckage.

When I woke up from the dream, the Lord started to speak to me and said that there was indeed a witch attacking me, but the curses she sent against me backfired on her instead. The Lord later confirmed that the witch would not be able to touch or harm me, and to not be afraid. Father further relayed that angels would be sent on assignment to assist and protect me.

All of this is not shocking. When I had this dream, the Lord raised up an intercessor to pray for me who has become a beloved sister in Christ. What I saw in the dream confirmed what the Lord showed her when praying for me. This sister had visions of a witch that kept her face hidden opposing me, but not only that, she saw that the witch was also trying to kill me. As she prayed for me, the Lord started to show her visions of me being in a terrible car crash and then she saw me in the hospital fighting for my life. Because of this, the sister in Christ started to pray more urgently for me.

But would you believe that around this same time I narrowly escaped being in a horrible car crash in reality? There were two situations specifically that occurred when I was travelling home from work. In one incident on the highway, I nearly collided with a silly driver who abruptly cut in front of me, but I managed to swerve out of the way in time and my vehicle went off the road. It just so happened that I was praying in tongues when this occurred, and the Holy Spirit kept me calm all the way. The second incident happened on the highway again, and I was nearly crushed by a 16-wheeler when trying to merge into a lane, but again I swerved away just in time. These weren't coincidences; they were outright attacks. You see, Satan and his people don't play fair.

In this same season, witchcraft reared its ugly head again. One evening I was in my home watching YouTube on my TV. I got up from my couch to go into the kitchen to make some tea. As I stood up, I saw a black figure out of the corner of my eye that quickly disappeared. I paused and noticed that the atmosphere of my home felt strange. When I finished making my tea, I headed back to the couch only to see the black outline of a human figure appear and disappear again. Only this time, the Holy Spirit urgently told me *"You're not alone in your home, someone else is here."* I immediately knew what this meant, and I started to pray, rebuke, and cut the silver cord (Ecclesiastes 12:6-7) of any person that entered my home. Someone had astral projected into my apartment (a good book to read and understand about this is *The Serpent and the Saviour* by Dave Bryan). What was strange about the whole thing is that at the time, I was in a prophetic intercessory group. This same witch had also astral projected into the homes of two other intercessors in the group. Everyone was put on high alert, and we increased in prayer.

During that time the Lord had me on a tight spiritual warfare routine. Because witches work along with monitoring spirits, he had me regularly bind all monitoring spirits that would seek to obtain and carry information about me. I was also instructed to pray against blood sacrifices and voodoo. Holy Spirit would also have me say two simple but very effective prayers and declarations: 1.) "I flood my home and environment with the blood of Jesus, in Jesus' name." 2.) "I drink the blood of Jesus, and I eat the flesh of Jesus."

The second prayer point came about because I also started to be attacked in my body. I would have dreams of me being sick and having a spirit of infirmity attached to me. Even though I would rebuke such dreams, afterwards, I would start to feel sick in my body. The Lord would then tell me to pray against viruses and illness, and afterwards I would start to physically feel better without taking any medication.

Another manifestation of witchcraft occurred still. On one particular shift at work, I was going about my job while listening to a pastor's sermon. Suddenly, I saw a literal black fiery ball appear before me, and it aggressively darted in my direction and tried to enter my body. I started to immediately pray in tounges as the Holy Spirit rose up in me and the black ball disappeared. After praying the Lord began to speak to me that the black fiery ball was a manifestation of witchcraft that certain people were trying to attack me with. So again, I was put on high alert by praying against evil altars and black magic.

Like many other Spirit-filled Believers, witchcraft was coming against me in some interesting ways. I'll share an additional dream with you that exposed another attack.

I was walking downtown in a city along a darkly lit street at night. I saw a crowd of people standing in the road and for some reason approached warily. Suddenly, a man dressed in black appeared before me aiming a handgun in my direction. He fired 3-4 bullets which hit me in my abdomen and chest. I crumpled to the asphalt ground and felt myself bleeding out. None of the people in the group I saw before attempted to assist me or call for help. Instead, they stood beside the perpetrator and watched me as I lay bleeding. In determined desperation, I simply prayed, "Lord, help me." After I uttered that prayer, a supernatural wave of healing overtook me, and I rose to my feet in anger. I darted in the direction of the man who shot me, and I started to beat him mercilessly. As I got him to the ground, I started to trample and stomp on his face and body until I saw his flesh ripping away in chunks and blood all over the ground. I continued to beat him until I knew he was dead, and no one attempted to stop me. Somehow the bullets hit me, and I bled, but I didn't die by the power of God.

When I woke up, the Lord revealed to me that the source of the attack in the dream was witchcraft. Father told me that it was a demon that shot at me in the dream, but the demonic spirit was unable to be successful in their mission against me. The bullets did not kill me, and I defeated the evil spirit that was sent. In the realm of the spirit, we can curse demons and gain the victory. The dream also reminded me of the words of David in Psalms:

"I will call upon the Lord, who is worthy to be praised:

so shall I be saved from mine enemies. The sorrows of death compassed me, and the floods of ungodly men made me afraid... I have pursued mine enemies, and overtaken them: neither did I turn again till they were consumed. I have wounded them that they were not able to rise: they are fallen under my feet. For thou hast girded me with strength unto the battle: thou hast subdued under me those that rose up against me." – **Psalm 18:3-4, 37-39**

The Lord also began to direct me more to the Book of Psalms for different warfare strategies against witchcraft. In particular, he highlighted Psalm 94 and 91 to me. I would regularly read and pray using the psalms as a way of offensively opposing witchcraft attacks released against me.

FIGHTING PRINCIPALITIES

When one thinks of principalities, we remember the story of the prophet Daniel whose angel had to combat the Prince of Persia. It is no coincidence that in Ephesians 6:12 Paul mentions that we fight against "...principalities and powers..." I have experienced what it is like to wrestle against a principality. These unseen entities govern the affairs of areas, regions, and territories.

In African, Caribbean, and Latin American culture, water or marine spirits are venerated and folklore is told about mermaids, mami wata, Oshun, Yemoja, or fish people. Such tales have been woven into the cultural fabric of storytelling from these regions, but many still view them from a mythological perspective. However, these fish-human hybrids (chimeras) or fish-gods do exist. They are evil spiritual entities that gain their power from the waters and entice humans into spiritual covenants that can last generations. Think of the god Dagon who was worshipped by the Philistines in the Bible (1 Samuel 5).

People who have African ancestry (like me) will often encounter and be afflicted by these entities (whether we know it or not). In the marine kingdom, there exists a hierarchy where these spiritual entities wield authority based on territory. One such principality is called "The Queen of the Coast". This Queen is a fallen angel responsible for regions that exist within the Atlantic Ocean, Caribbean Sea, the Gulf of Mexico, the Bermuda Triangle, and more. She rules over coastal lands and areas. She is a wicked principality that governs trade, transportation, prostitution, spiritual and sexual perversion, financial transactions, idolatry, false religions, human trafficking, witchcraft, and many others in the regions which she has authority over. In West Africa, she is known to many ministers who have encountered her. If you want to know more about this particular principality, then I recommend the book called *The Queen of the Coast* by Prayer Madueke.

Now, during one the roughest seasons of my walk, I experienced some very difficult spiritual warfare. Because of everything that happened I had fallen into depression again and was struggling internally. God had to especially minister to me during this time, because I was growing weary with experiencing spiritual attack after attack. I was so overwhelmed in the battle. That was until one night I was praying and the Lord said to me, "*The Queen of the Coast is attacking you.*" After he said this, I paused. I immediately knew who he meant when he mentioned this evil entity. I was like, "Lord, I've never come against this principality. I have not operated in the spirit against her without license or crossed any boundaries I was not meant to." Father's response was simple: *"The devil hates you, doesn't want you to walk in the fullness of your calling, and is using this principality to trouble you."* I knew he was right.

The Holy Spirit then gave me detailed instructions on how to navigate this principality's oppositional attacks upon my life. Her attacks against me looked like this:

- Demonic night visions and dreams (especially dreams of unclean and sexual things)
- Increased dreams of water bodies, marine entities, and serpentine spirits
- Increased surveillance by monitoring spirits
- Increased witchcraft attacks and curses
- Financial issues and blockages
- Mental health struggles (depression, anxiety, confusion)
- Relationship struggles
- Increased instances of rejection and loneliness
- Increased situational frustration, delay, and disappointment

God gave me strategies to deal with the opposition from this principality:

- Anoint myself daily
- Pray specifically against marine witchcraft and spirits
- Pray more intentionally before going to sleep (especially praying in tongues)
- Bind up monitoring, witchcraft, and water spirits

- Ask God for angelic assistance against the principality
- Pray intently over my destiny
- Trust in God despite the frustration

When I started to do these things consistently, I began to achieve breakthrough. I was obedient as God fought for me against this spiritual entity. I noticed that the attacks waned whenever I would put these things into practice, but when I lapsed or got too busy and forgot to do some of these things, the attacks would pickup again. The Queen of the Coast is a strong principality, so there was also always backlash that I had to fight against too. I can say for a surety that God gave me grace to fight. Consider one of my dreams:

I was on a tour bus with some travellers, and we were headed to some kind of university campus. As the bus moved, it started to travel on a road along a coast, and I could see the sea out of one of the windows. I observed that the sea was calm but also looked grey and mysterious. Then my eyes beheld sitting on the sea a blue-green statue that had three mermaids in an odd configuration. One of the mermaids in the statue had a conch shell to her mouth as if she was blowing it. Suddenly, as the bus continued traveling, I heard a piercing noise (like some sort of horn blast). As I heard the sound, I saw the mermaids in the statue come to life and become living, breathing organisms. These mermaids headed from out of the sea toward the coast, walking on two legs. The bus then veered off the coastal road and made its way to the beach. The people on the bus I was traveling with disembarked and started congregating on the beach in anticipation of the mermaids. However, I was hesitant to get off knowing what these creatures were, but eventually I did. The mermaids met with the group of people who had now

formed a line. Each person in the line approached the mermaids and received gifts from them like various seafood and treasures from the sea. I was not in the line and was very uncomfortable, but I then started to pray and bind up the marine spirits and powers. As I started to quietly pray, I saw one of the mermaids who had a fishing rod in her hand (she was the mermaid pulling up treasures and seafood from the sea to give to the people) begin to struggle to pull up her catch. The fishing rod in her hand began to put up resistance and started to malfunction, and I knew it was doing so because of my prayers. Suddenly, the mermaids started to look around and ask the group of people, "who is doing that?!" Although I remained silent and no one else responded, one of the mermaids locked eyes with me and pointed in my direction saying, "it's you." I froze into position wondering what was next. She looked at me and told me that she needed to show me something. As the people were receiving their gifts from the waters, she led me down a staircase that led into the sea floor where I could still breathe. She started to show me things under the sea, like the mermaids' base. I just looked and observed as she spoke. Afterwards, she led me up from the staircase to the beach. I took nothing from the mermaids, but everyone else had entered back into the bus. I heard the same horn blast from earlier, and this time, I saw the mermaids return into the waters and they formed back into a statue seated on the sea. I entered the bus, and we continued along the coastal road.

This was a very interesting but intense dream. When I woke up, I was rather intrigued. The dream showed that through prayer, I was able to disrupt the operation of these marine spirits and because of that, they had a fear of me and what I could do. Although they made covenants with the people who formed the line (by accepting their gifts), I took nothing from them, knowing that there would be an evil consequence. But because of the power I showed in the dream, the mermaid that led me down the staircase into the sea wanted me to see what was down below.

Coastal powers are evil powers. The new city where I lived had a lake and beaches, so I was in the jurisdiction of the Queen of the Coast. God began to show me that her attacks were because of the call on my life and my prayers.

Another principality I've had to endure attacks from has been Leviathan, the ancient sea monster described by God in Job 41. Leviathan is a principality that is over many nations, states, provinces, and cities. He is the "king over all the children of pride." So, you can imagine I've had to battle him in the workplace, church, and in general society. Coincidentally, Leviathan works together well with Jezebel (which is a strong spirit that loves to attack prophetic people). To battle Leviathan, I have learned to do the opposite of what he likes – assume gracious humility, consult the Lord on every decision, and fervently pray. God is the only one who can deal with the power of Leviathan, so the Holy Spirit has always protected me and given me strategies against him.

DEALING WITH DEMONIZED PEOPLE

My career thus far has involved taking care of people. I've had jobs that require me to see the good, bad, and ugly in human beings from the smallest to the greatest. I've seen what pharmaceuticals can do to the brain. I've witnessed demons manifest and take a person's tiny body and turn it into a lethal weapon. I've observed how some of the errors of modern psychiatry and medical treatment can have detrimental effects on people. Because of my work and the requirement for me to build rapport and connections with people, I have experienced opposition from the enemy.

On one particular weekend, I was registered to participate in a deliverance teaching conference through a local church ministry. The Lord had opened the door for me to attend this conference so I could be trained in deliverance ministry. It just so happened that I was also slated to work the night shift on the Friday night into the Saturday morning before commuting to participate in the learning session. Being that I had worked with a particular client all that week and was under a lot of stress, I thought nothing of it when I started to experience a painful throb in my right calf. I brushed it off at the onset of my shift, but as the time progressed the pain started to intensify and my calf which had been its normal size a few hours ago had ballooned and became badly swollen. I ended my shift limping into the car and began to cry out to the Lord as I made my way to the conference location. The Lord began to speak to me that what was happening was demonic, so I began to pray while driving in pain.

Once I arrived at the conference, the man of God who was ministering that day took one look at me and called me over. After I greeted him, he asked me why I was limping and grimacing. I told him I started experiencing pain in my right calf during my night shift and it had intensified greatly on my way to the session. The man of God, who I'll call Minister Bob, got a chair for me to sit down, and both him and another intercessor immediately started to pray for me. As they began to pray, Minister Bob received a word of knowledge about soul ties causing an open door for this attack. However, I was confused. I thought all of the evil soul ties I had made in the past were broken (I broke each and every one). But Minister Bob told me it was a recently made soul tie between myself and one of my clients as he inquired of the Lord.

Because much of my job entails caring for other people and relies on building connections, it becomes easy to create soul ties (think of David and Jonathan – they had a soul tie as they were incredibly good friends; 1 Samuel 18:1-4). People think that soul ties can only be created via sexual interactions, but this is not the case. Soul ties can exist due to emotional connections and social bonds with people as well. In fact, people can have soul ties to other people, things, places, and events. The soul is made of the mind, will, and emotions; when this is understood, it makes understanding how soul ties can be made easier. The soul tie I had was created by caring for a client who was demonized (oppressed by demonic spirits), which had allowed demons of destruction, pain, and death to afflict my body.

Minister Bob walked me through breaking the soul tie and the curses that it caused, and then he laid hands on the painful area of my calf. I felt the presence of God overtake in that moment and felt as if a spiritual salve was placed on that part of my body. The best way I can describe it is this: I felt a cool healing sensation begin to remove all the demonic garbage that was causing the acute pain I had (like if a light bandage with medicine on it had been applied). It was all spiritual. The swelling immediately began to go down and I was finally able to start walking properly again (and this was all before the conference had even started). I started to thank and praise God.

The Lord started to teach me that because of my work; I would have to do spiritual warfare to destroy attacks from the enemy through clients. The enemy would use clients and soul ties to foster spiritual opposition against me. Many people who are Christian working in similar fields often experience some of the things that I'm talking about. Certain work positions require elevated levels of spiritual warfare.

It was through spiritual opposition that I learned how to be scourged; one of the most painful lessons on this chosen journey.

13 | THE SCOURGING

"For our light affliction, which is but for a moment, worketh for us a far more exceeding and eternal weight of glory."
2 Corinthians 4:17

What was it like for Jesus to be scourged? It must have been unimaginably painful, even to the deepest core. As Christians who expect to look like Christ at the end of our journey, we then should expect to be scourged like him too. The problem is this topic isn't popular and therefore not often preached. Apostle Paul stated in Galatians 6:17 that he bared in his body the marks of Christ. The marks he was speaking of weren't necessarily just physical, but also spiritual. He went through something for believing and actively participating in the mission of the Gospel of Jesus Christ, that caused him pain and cost him something. It was the pain and cost that was the scourging. It comes in tests, trials, temptations, and afflictions. If your Christianity has cost you nothing, then your faith has very little value.

God is looking for people that will have a faith in Him so absolute that they are willing to pay the high price. People want to be called but not scourged. People want to be anointed but not scourged. People want to be gifted but not scourged. People want to prophesy but not scourged. People want to cast out demons but not scourged. People want to perform miracles but not scourged. They want a Gospel and Christian faith that costs them nothing. They want it easy. And ease is not the way to be fully and wholly used by God. So, then the question is, are you willing to be scourged? Jesus was willing, he said, "*…nevertheless not my will, but thine, be done.*" (Luke 22:42)

According to the Cambridge Dictionary:

SCOURGE / Verb –

"To cause great suffering or a lot of trouble."

Probably the hardest part of being a chosen one is the scourging. It's the picking apart to be put back together again that hurts the most. And unfortunately for our flesh, it is also the most necessary thing in order to answer God's call and become an effective Kingdom ambassador and labourer. To truly understand why we need to be scourged through sharing in the sufferings of Christ, we need to know that the scourging is not about us. The scourging is about the lives, destines, and generations that will be impacted and transformed due to our obedience, persistence, and yielding. It is all for the glory. And that's exactly what we learned from Jesus' example.

> "Looking unto Jesus the author and finisher of our faith; who for the joy that was set before him endured the cross, despising the shame, and is set down at the right hand of the throne of God. For consider him that endured such contradiction of sinners against himself, lest ye be wearied and faint in your minds." – **Hebrews 12:2-3**

Jesus Christ went through his own scourging – being betrayed, tortured, and crucified for the joy that he saw before him in you and me being saved. For the joy of our deliverance and redemption. For the joy of his chosen people arising in their callings and shaking the wicked out of the earth. For the joy of defeating Satan. For the joy of reconciling to his creation. For the joy of banishing evil. It wasn't about the God-man's scourging per se, it was all about what would occur after it.

Likewise, the chosen one must remember that his/her scourging is not about the suffering or pain, but about what comes after and the joy of it all. The things that come after scourging are ministries being birthed, revival in people's lives, deliverance from strongholds and demons, healing of bodies, hearts, and souls, and the resilience and endurance required to walk with God until the end.

One of the most fascinating women of God I've heard of is Kathryn Kuhlman. She was an American televangelist who was noted to have a ministry filled with the manifestation of miracles and God's healing power. Like any other saint, during her lifetime she made mistakes, some of which were publicly known. But to the glory of God, she ended her chosen journey as a stalwart of the faith. One of the best quotes about the chosen one's scourging was stated by her: "Do you want to know what the anointing will cost? Do you really want to know? It will cost you everything."

The 'cost' that Ms. Kuhlman was speaking of is the scourging. It is God's requirement for consecration and greater glory. It's the heavy price of not having things your way but allowing God to have his way. To do that takes mature humility. The price is paid through rejection, occasional isolation, crucifying the flesh by giving up certain wants and desires, losses, and often feeling misunderstood in this world of sin. The cost is the merger of a crushing and a healing altogether. Only those who've experienced it know what I mean.

It is also easy to become discouraged during this phase. However, the enemy uses discouragement to remove our focus from the assignment God has given us. The enemy will send discouraging words via family members, friends, employers, pastors, spiritual advisors, and even some who claim to be discerning Christians. Your job is to ensure your relationship with God is so tight via Holy Spirit, that your trust in him and his agenda for your life, calling, and purpose cannot be shaken. The only way to overcome discouragement is by knowing and trusting Jesus. You must contend for what God has promised you. Fight for it!

While the scourging is nothing to be afraid of, it is a season of the chosen one's journey that will require total surrender to God. It makes our hearts tender and pliable so our Heavenly Father can use us. God, with the assistance of the Holy Spirit, will carry a chosen one through this period. It will not be easy, but it will be worth it. God will leave us to make the decision. Will we suffer the cost, or not?

> "Then said Jesus unto his disciples, If any man will come after me, let him deny himself, and take up his cross, and follow me. For whosoever will save his life shall lose it: and whosoever will lose his life for my sake shall find it." – **Matthew 16:24-25**

Here's a good question to test your intentions with God: **what would you willingly give up to follow after Jesus?**

In Matthew chapter 19, we see a rich young man was unable to part with his wealth and possessions to follow the King of Kings. He asked Jesus what he needed to do to have eternal life. Jesus told the lad that he should follow the commandments. But when the young man said he already followed the commandments, Jesus introduced him to the concept of true sacrifice (the cost) – a concept he appeared unable to come to terms with.

> "Jesus answered him, "If you wish to be perfect [that is, have the spiritual maturity that accompanies godly character with no moral or ethical deficiencies], go and sell what you have and give [the money] to the poor, and you will have treasure in heaven; and come, follow Me [becoming My disciple, believing and trusting in Me and walking the same path of life that I walk]."
> But when the young man heard this, he left grieving and distressed, for he owned much property and had many possessions [which he treasured more than his relationship with God]." – **Matthew 19:21-22 (AMP)**

Some people will never achieve greater glory in their lives as Christians, simply because they're not ready or willing to give up things (possessions, relationships, mindsets, plans, careers, etc.) that God requires them to. Then there are those who are so overzealous in their pursuit of God, that they forget an important part of Believing in Jesus is counting the cost (Luke 14:28). Indeed, count the cost and count it well (the true cost).

My Scourging

Here is where I state a truth most people don't know about me. For most of my 20s thus far, I have been completely unhappy. What was alarming was that I didn't realise this fact. It's not like I tried to avoid the truth or deny it; I was just too busy and caught up to notice it. I met Jesus at 20. That means that for most of my adult life, I've been living in unhappiness. People didn't see my tears and I didn't share my pain. There was just a profound sadness I learned to live with.

One night as I prayed on my bed, the Holy Spirit in a tone of concern said, "*You are not happy.*" It was a very fatherly and matter-of-factly thing to say. Completely sobering, but it was true. And I just sobbed at understanding how true it was.

For me, being scourged has been a very painful exercise. It led to the revelation from God about my state of unhappiness. What I will dispel here is that our happiness or unhappiness does not determine our faith in God, nor does it negate God's goodness. Our faith must be pegged to something more solid than our feelings, emotions, and desires. But God was telling me I was unhappy for a reason.

Earlier in chapter 6, I mentioned how God told me that following him would cost me everything. In the scourging season I realised he was giving me a heads-up as I saw this part of the journey unfold before me. Following him has cost me so much. For the sake of purpose, following Jesus has cost me friendships, relationships, opportunities, and comforts. I've been talked about and slandered by people behind my back. I've endured hardships and many struggles. I have indeed *suffered*.

My unhappiness was not caused by following the Lord. It was caused by the weight of all the things I have been through. To be honest I felt very alone at times which only further contributed to this, especially when so many people surrounding me had no understanding or knowledge of what I was going through.

STRESS (FEAR & ANXIETY)

After graduating from university, I was instantly put into survival mode. I had to find work and housing quickly to support myself, as I recognised none of my relatives in Canada would help me. God was kind to me as he told me where to go, where to live, and what jobs to take. However, I was also faced with the struggle of immigrating and further integrating into a country whose culture, environment, and systems I wasn't fully familiar with. The fact that I did this on my own without much assistance from outside sources is a testament to God's goodness. I had to walk by faith and sustain immense pressure.

In this country, I have often worked 2-3 jobs with very little space for a good social life. COVID also had a huge impact on me because I became more withdrawn. For a very long time it was work-sleep-school-work-sleep-repeat, with bits of church and other occasional fellowship in between. This cyclical routine was absolutely suffocating, especially since I desired better. My nerves were fried, and I was always on edge, consumed with worry about sometimes even meeting my basic needs.

I would often cry myself to sleep after praying. My heart was critically shattered. Everything was on me, and keeping up with multiple demands with no help was hard. Most of the people that gained any semblance of understanding of what was going on with me at the time weren't even Christian. There was stress about immigration status; stress about money; stress about job and industry; stress concerning clients; stress about living environments; stress about family; stress from spiritual warfare; and stress about my own expectations. It seemed I was in a tight vacuum of pressure on every side. After successfully clearing one hurdle, the next challenge would appear quickly.

At the height of all of this going on, the Holy Spirit remained my constant Comforter and Helper. As I cried out to him, he uttered these words to me – *"Withstand it. Withstand the pressure. It will not hurt you. I have your back."* Diamonds that dazzle on fine jewelry pieces were created in an environment of pressure, which transformed carbon atoms into highly valued precious stone. Holy Spirit was teaching me that I was the diamond being made. He was incubating me, allowing me to go through pressure to ensure that the things that existed within me in a spiritually atomic state, would bear fruit and form into something beautiful. Sounds poetic, eh? I'm sure it does, but it didn't feel poetic or comfortable in the thick of it. I'm sure Jesus felt the pressure of his own scourging too; there's a reason why he started to sweat blood in Gethsemane.

What God intends and what we feel in the moment as we live out his intentions are two completely different things. Imagine even being stressed at church. While still living at my old apartment and dealing with Mike, I started attending a Pentecostal African church. At first things were going well. Then, I slowly began to get more and more angered by going. I shouldn't have been angry, but

I was. I was active in the church, became part of the young adults' group and spearheaded a quarterly Christian youth magazine. But in a sea of people who looked much like me, and believed in the same God I did, I had never felt so alone or unseen. That's because I was in a church that cared more about culture than Kingdom, and I was not growing spiritually or in my gifting by attending. The restlessness I could feel by not growing made me anxious, and I was stressed trying to relate to some of the attending members. I was an outsider even amongst "God's people".

There was also stress from expectations I put on myself and from trying to navigate the path God had for me. Stress about not knowing what comes next. Stress about not being good enough, or having enough resources financially, spiritually, and physically to make it. I remember laying on my bed in a tiring fit of anxiety, not being able to even function well because I was stressed about several events in my life. An overwhelming sense of panic would seek to overtake me, that Holy Spirit would then have to coach me out of. I was trying so hard to make everything work on my own that there was a level of pressure I was solely responsible for. God had to draw me away from this thinking and help me to depend on him for *everything*. It took a while for me to grasp and extend my trust in the Lord. When I tried to depend on myself and my own understanding, that's when stress and anxiety increased. Only true peace came when I followed what God said, and he constantly reminded me of his word in Proverbs 3:5-6.

FRUSTRATION AND DISAPPOINTMENT

Everything that I had imagined my future to be as an ambitious and intelligent young woman was disrupted and diverted. All the dreams that I had before my eyes for my life, somehow, God was telling me that these were not part of the path he had for me. It wasn't the fact that God was telling me, "*No*", "*Not yet*", "*Not them*". It was the wondering of *when will it happen?* The "it" I'm speaking of here is the breakthrough that I so desperately needed. I had waited and endured so much. My question each time was, "Lord, *when?*" All the Holy Spirit would repeatedly tell me was, "*The best is yet to come.*" So, when was this "best" going to come?

I had planned to build a career in science or the trades. But the Lord was telling me to build a career in media and sent me back to school. I had planned to be married by 25. But the Lord was telling me, "*There's someone better out there for you.*" My plan was to go back home to Barbados if things got any worse. God's plan was for me to stay in Canada and weather the storm under his guiding hand. I had planned to switch fields after 2 years. The Lord's plan was to keep me in the social services field for over 5 years. I had planned to move to a different province. But God's plan was for me to remain in the province he initially put me in.

There was disappointment after disappointment. Things I expected to go one way ended up going another. Losses that I took in absolute silence with a grace that only the Lord could give. I was frustrated with where I was at; maybe a growing sense of discontentment that the Lord had to address in me. For years I sat back and cheered on my peers, old school mates, and new acquaintances as they seemingly 'flew' in life. I saw them build successful careers, get married, have kids, travel, and obtain various achievements and I was genuinely elated for them, but an ache continued to grow inside me. I had come to know this ache too well; it had become familiar to me. The ache was pain – borne from frustration and disappointment. I hid it so well. Because quite frankly, who would actually care?

With the number of gifts, talents, credentials, and ambition I had – I should have been further, I thought. I felt how Job must've felt – knowing that he had it all at one point, and then it was snatched from him in an instant with only pain as the result. I was in pain because I knew my potential and that what resided in me would take me very far. I knew the path that the Lord showed me I should take would lead to overwhelming success, and I chose this path and all it came with. I just wondered, *when*. It felt like dying inside. The scripture that best describes the effect of such frustration and disappointment is this:

> "Hope deferred maketh the heart sick: but when the desire cometh, it is a tree of life." – **Proverbs 13:12**

With all the tears I cried, I should have been swimming in a pool. Some may be seeking to read specifics, but I will not indulge them. Some things are best left unsaid. I sat back and watched as people tried to gain insight. Sat back and heard the judgements made in error about my character, path, and faith. They had no clue what I was going through, and I made them none the wiser. The psalmist only too well put my emotions into words:

> "My soul [as well as my body] is greatly dismayed. But as for You, O LORD—how long [until You act on my behalf]? I am weary with my groaning; Every night I

soak my bed with tears, I drench my couch with my weeping." – **Psalm 6:3,6 (AMP)**

When I was near my breaking point in 2022 and 2023, the Lord started to seriously talk to me. He would continually echo his Word back to me:

> "Except the LORD build the house, they labour in vain that build it: except the LORD keep the city, the watchman waketh but in vain." – **Psalm 127:1**

Over and over again the words of this psalm would be pushed into my mind. Here the Lord was reminding me that I had to let go of and forget everything that I thought I knew and wanted and allow him to build the life he had for me from scratch for His glory. Part of the frustration was trying to figure things out on my own, but that wasn't what God wanted. He continued to lovingly redirect me. I had to let go and let God – and it was *hard* – but I did it by faith and grace.

Quaintly put: *"Temporary pain for permanent glory, Camille,"* said the Holy Spirit. We don't understand that glory has a weight to it. To obtain and function in the glory, we must be able to carry and handle the weight of it while trusting God. How do I know this? Because the Lord mentions it in his Word. Repeatedly, the Holy Spirit would remind me of the *"weight of glory."*

> "For our light affliction, which is but for a moment, worketh for us a far more exceeding and eternal weight of glory; While we look not at the things which are seen, but at the things which are not seen: for the things which are seen are temporal; but the things which are not seen are eternal." – **2 Corinthians 4:17-18**

Interestingly, the chapter that contained those verses the Lord kept referring me to, was Paul describing his ministry and the hard things the apostles had to experience for the glory. Everything that was happening to me was occurring for a reason. And the reason was simply stated by the Lord himself: *"You will soon start ministry. So, PUSH."* When I was at my lowest, the Lord stirred up a woman of God to start earnestly praying for me. She had sensed the pain, fatigue, and weariness in me in the spirit, and the Lord moved her to start praying. She called me one day and said, "You are called as a five-fold minister. But you must PUSH past pain. PUSH past the depression. And as a mother gives birth to her baby, you will have to PUSH until this ministry is birthed. It is working together for your good." So, I did just that. I began to *push*. Despite everything, I endeavoured to begin a personal revival.

"Lord, I don't know how much more I can take," I cried.

"*PUSH, Camille,*" said Holy Spirit.

"Father, I feel so weak. I'm not where I should be, and everything is too heavy," I said.

"*PUSH. I'm cheering you on,*" echoed Holy Spirit. He continued, "*I know your path has been rough and you've been through a lot. But I allowed it because I know you can handle it. At the end of it, you will be stronger. You have a high calling. Keep pushing.*"

Are you ready to serve God unless you've been brought to breaking point? I think not. And that's exactly why it was important for me to push. By pushing, I also had to learn how to grieve. People think that grieving is only done when you lose a loved one. But I've learned through the scourging that grieving takes on another aspect. I had to grieve my old desires, dreams, and plans. I had to grieve lost relationships and opportunities that were not meant for me. To grieve wanting to justify myself from strangers' opinions of me. Grief is a part of the scourging.

The Lord then began to show me that the unhappiness I had was due to the suffering I had been called to endure to pay the price. Anyone who constantly encounters disappointment, frustration, stress, loneliness, grief, and spiritual warfare would be unhappy. It was a human response to spiritual and life conditions. Father told me I needed to find my joy again, and I really did. He began to give me joy in doses. Joy in smiling. Joy during long walks and listening to music. Joy in his promises being kept. Joy in singing. Joy in writing. The imbalance was not endless, and the overwhelming feelings began to be destroyed. He replaced everything I lost with his salve of hope. One of the prayers I prayed during this time was, "Lord, repay me for everything I've lost and redeem my time according to your word in Joel 2:25, in Jesus' name." I believe Jesus has answered that prayer, restoring joy and happiness to me.

The conclusion I've reached is that no part of our lives, including the scourging, is wasted on our journey. These incidents and moments fit together like puzzle pieces creating a destiny-aligning path that was always meant to be.

14 | THE JOURNEY

"He hath shewed thee, O man, what is good; and what doth the LORD require of thee, but to do justly, and to love mercy, and to walk humbly with thy God?"
Micah 6:8

For each of the called and chosen, a journey has been crafted by God in the heavenly realms before the foundations of the earth were laid. Almighty God has a wonderful administrative power attributed to his divinity. Yahweh is the best record-keeper and data analyst to ever exist. He has libraries in the heavens with books filled with prophetic text about our lives. Our journeys and destinies are written in these books from our very conception to our last breath. This life in Christ is a beautifully woven story. God is honestly the best author there is. He knows every character, has written the best lines, and has developed the greatest redemptive story arcs. It is therefore the chosen one's job to consult the Lord about each chapter and paragraph as we navigate this Christ-walk.

Our journey in Jesus Christ is a collection of our triumphs, sorrows, battles, successes, and tribulations, which form a unique testimony that we can share with others. Most of our journey really has nothing to do with us individually but has to do with what God wants to accomplish through us. Our journey, our destiny, and our purpose are all interconnected, and can be fully manifested when we accept Jesus into our lives and live for him.

There is a book in heaven about your journey as a chosen one. How do I know this? The scriptures give me an indication.

> "Then those who feared the LORD [with awe-filled reverence] spoke to one another; and the LORD paid attention and heard it, and a book of remembrance was written before Him of those who fear the LORD [with an attitude of reverence and respect] and who esteem His name." – **Malachi 3:16 (AMP)**

> "You have taken account of my wanderings; Put my tears in Your bottle. Are they not recorded in Your book?" – **Psalms 56:8 (AMP)**

How we navigate this journey will depend on our obedience, determination, and relationship with God. It is also important to have God guide us through every step of our journey. He will be our biggest cheerleader, confidante, and friend on this wonderful path.

There are five things chosen ones must remember on their journey:

1.) Be led by the Spirit of God.

> "For as many as are led by the Spirit of God, they are the sons of God." – **Romans 8:14**

2.) Honour God in everything you do – this will yield bountiful results.

"And whatsoever ye do in word or deed, do all in the name of the Lord Jesus, giving thanks to God and the Father by him**." – Colossians 3:17**

3.) Be steadfast in faith.

"But without faith it is impossible to please him: for he that cometh to God must believe that he is, and that he is a rewarder of them that diligently seek him." **– Hebrews 11:6**

4.) Advance in the spirit and in life by attending to the spiritual laws outlined in scripture.

"Observe the requirements of the Lord your God, and follow all his ways. Keep the decrees, commands, regulations, and laws written in the Law of Moses so that you will be successful in all you do and wherever you go." **– 1 Kings 2:3**

5.) Know that this life is not your end; there is another life to come which this journey prepares us for.

"And this is the promise that he hath promised us, even eternal life." **– 1 John 2:25**

What do *you* think God has written about you?

Dr. Myles Munroe also said something that I think every chosen one should make note of concerning their journey. He was a Bahamian pastor who had an incredible teaching gift and ministry. In his wisdom, he expressed these words:

"The wealthiest place in the world is not the gold mines of South America or the oil fields of Iraq or Iran. They are not the diamond mines of South Africa or the banks of the world. The wealthiest place on the planet is just down the road. It is the cemetery. There lie buried companies that were never started, inventions that were never made, bestselling books that were never written, and masterpieces that were never painted. In the

cemetery is buried the greatest treasure of untapped potential."

As a chosen one, you should be determined to leave this earth absolutely empty. When you depart, there should be nothing left to give. All of your gifts, talents, knowledge, and wisdom should be fully expended and used. Everything that God created and purposed you to do should be completed. The order of the chosen should be:

No. 1 – Find Jesus,

No. 2 – Find your purpose; and,

No. 3 – Execute the destiny God has for you.

The grave that you lay in at your end should never be seen as a wealthy place. The treasure you've gained along your journey should have its place in heaven, along with a world that saw and experienced the fruit of your life and the legacy you left behind.

God desires our journey with him to be a faithful walk to the end. In this way he can utter these words to us in finality: *"Well done, my good and faithful servant."* (Matthew 25:23).

To be chosen means that you too must choose. Will you choose God's path or your own way? Will you choose abundant life or the staleness of death? Will you choose Godly success over earthly success? Or will you choose eternal life over eternal death? Heaven or hell? Our chosen journey is tethered to a choice we will have to make every single day: To love Jesus with our whole heart, mind, soul and strength, and to love our neighbour as ourselves; picking up and carrying our cross in surrender to the Holy King. It is a journey of sacrifice, because God the Father sacrificed his most precious thing on our behalf – his only begotten Son.

Walk the journey out, continually allowing yourself to abide in God's presence. It is the only way to ascend, and the only way to see his light at our conclusion. The chosen journey is a small part of the echo of time. What is most important is that Master Jesus is watching over our every step – that's what makes it successful.

> "Then they said, "Ask God whether or not our journey will be successful." "Go in peace," the priest replied. "For the Lord is watching over your journey."" **– Judges 18:5-6 (NLT)**

My Journey

If I died today, I think I'd be alright. But I am not destined to die as yet, and even if I did die, I would still be alive. That's the hope I've been assured of through Christ Jesus. There are too many people walking the earth who simply do not have this same assurance. They haven't made their minds up yet or refuse to choose the Lord and his way. But my journey is bound up in persuading men for Lord Yeshua and Yahweh. This is why I live the way I do. Why I stand for holiness. Why I firmly am a promoter of the Gospel of Jesus Christ. And, also, why I've written this book.

I believe I'm only in the first few chapters of my journey with the Lord. There are still many more chapters I have left to go. And some of these chapters are eternal.

You may have read and found my journey to be insignificant, and that would be your opinion to have. To me, my journey with Jesus has been the cornerstone of my life. I have made up my mind to follow Jesus as my Lord and Saviour, and I cannot turn back – I don't want to. Who I am as a chosen one is beyond my wildest dreams. I know what it's like to be angry, wayward, confused, immoral, deceived, and manipulated by the evil powers of the spiritual world. The Camille I am now is more circumspect, focused, a lover of truth, principled, and free. I don't want to be in darkness, neither do I desire the things of this world – they can do nothing for me. The transformation I have undergone has been radical, and the people that know me best know this to be true. There is no cogent explanation for me living out the chosen journey. It is only by the Spirit.

I have witnessed God's power firsthand. I have tasted and known the goodness of the Lord. I have sat at the table of the Holy Spirit and gleaned from his presence. I know that there is a God who exists outside of time that has caused this world to come into being, and who loves humanity dearly. And because he lavished his love on me, he wants to use me to share that same love with my fellowman.

So, the only question left is: what's next? And that question can only be answered by what currently is.

I think my entire journey so far can be summed up in one Bible verse. The verse is found in the Book of Job which has become one of my favourite books in the Word to read.

> "Then, even if your beginnings were modest, your final days will be full of prosperity." – **Job 8:7 (HCSB)**

I am certain that this verse is applied to my own chosen journey and so many others' as well. Though I started my journey with very little; though I have been driven to modest means; though I've been through much pain and rejection; though I've cried so many tears; though I almost gave up; though I have trauma I don't often speak of – *yet* in these days and the ones to come I shall be prosperous, I shall increase, and I shall be enlarged by the hand of God. Not only me, but also my house. One of my names is Gedaliah as mentioned in this book, and that means greatness and success has no choice but to locate me and mine as spoken by the mouth of God. God's Word **must** come to pass in my life, in Jesus' name.

The chosen journey I'm on was made to inspire others to live for the Lord. Who are the others I speak of? Well, the "others" are the chosen ones who have yet to come to an understanding of who they are and who God created them to be. These chosen ones are part of a generation that our mothers and fathers could only have imagined. They are giants in the spirit, called and set apart for these Last Days.

While I was in an intense season and fasting and praying, God gave me a prophetic word that has made me excited for the days to come concerning the chosen ones. This is what Holy Spirit told me:

> *"The Davids are coming. The sons of God who care for me, my word, and my law. Zechariahs shall arise – the people of God. They'll break some hedges. They'll crush the enemies. The devil is a liar. I'll show them the way. They dare to follow me. Make way! They will turn people's hearts back to me. Calebs shall come. The Kingdom shall come and arise. The satanic cults shall be scattered; they will be slain. I will break them."*

Basically, there is a generation in these Last Days who will pursue God wholeheartedly on this chosen journey. Like David (meaning "beloved") they will chase after God's very own heart and have a deep relationship with Yahweh. They will also war and conquer in the spirit even as David did on the battlefield. Their worship and anointing will drive out evil before them. Like Zechariah (meaning "YHWH remembers"), they will rebuild broken down walls and temple ruins from the generations of old; prophesying the Word of the Lord in power and might, causing those who hear to remember the ways of the Lord. And, like Caleb (meaning "faithful" or "brave"), they will be of a different spirit, not moved by fear of men or circumstance, but moved alone by the boldness of the fear of God, and maintaining their faithfulness to Yeshua. I am a part of this generation, and, if you see yourself reflected in the pages of what I've written in this book, you are a part of this generation too.

Here's what I have learned on my chosen journey so far that I'd like to share with you.

Learn to Trust God's Process

God is in the business of carrying us through this journey step by step. Our impatience does not offend or move him – he expects it because we are human. There were several times along this journey thus far where I have lost patience and grown anxious due to wanting things to move faster. Countless times I found myself praying and asking God why my training was taking so long and why the opposition was so tough; why I always felt displaced and out of sorts. Trusting him took so much out of me. Trusting God sometimes felt like I was losing a part of myself – and I was. I was losing the part of me that required to always understand.

Only until this part of me was dealt with could I truly trust him. When I trusted him, he came through for me in unexpected ways. He made me a citizen in a country that I was not born in because he said that I would do ministry there (solidifying his word to me). He elevated me to spaces and rooms I couldn't have imagined being in. God took hold of me in a barren place and gave me a bountiful return. I had to trust the process. He didn't lead me astray, and he continues to prove this to me as I fellowship with him on the journey. An additional part of trusting God's process was not comparing my journey with another person's. Comparing destroys our focus on divine assignments and God's plans. Focus on your own journey, working out your own salvation with fear and trembling. Every chosen one's journey will not look the same.

Increase in Understanding

God wants us to understand him, this life, and the world he's placed us to live in. We can't walk this journey well and be stagnant or resistant to deepening our understanding. In the Book of Proverbs, there is a command to continually obtain understanding (Proverbs 4:7). I believe there is a reason for that. So many things in life simply won't make sense no matter how hard we try to understand them. When we get stumped, we then need a higher form understanding that comes from the counsel of God through his Word and Spirit.

Along my journey, I have found understanding to be my friend. By grasping the wisdom in the scriptures and via Holy Ghost, I have been able to obtain and expand in the area of discernment. Discernment on multiple occasions has saved me in so many different ways. I have been able to discern people, spirits, origins of situations, and knowings of the future. We need understanding and discernment to withstand the satanic onslaught that these Last Days will bring, and they will strengthen our relationship with God on the journey.

Navigate Relationships Accordingly

If there's anything to know about God, know that he has a deep love for people (his creation). Because he loves people, he wants his chosen ones to love them too. One of the ways to give and receive God's love is through relationships with others. On this chosen journey, we cannot be successful without other people. Lot needed Abraham. David needed Jonathan. Elisha needed Elijah. Samuel needed Eli. Peter needed Jesus. Paul needed Silas. Timothy needed Paul. God will give us connections and relationships that we'll need to steward and honour. Destiny helpers via connections and relationships can transform our vision, purpose, and journey. When it comes to people, I always thought I was bad at interacting with others. I found myself to be too awkward and independent when it came to connecting with folks, to the point where I never thought people would ever "get" me. But God sent some beautiful Kingdom people who began to understand me not by looking exteriorly but viewing me from the spirit. They saw my passion, drive, independence, creativity, and humility that others couldn't see, and they also called this out so that I could see it too. Much of where I am today is because of people I've met on this journey.

I've started to honour the beautiful relationships God has given me, and I've been able to share God's love with others because that's what he wants. Our journeys will be defined by how we served God by serving and loving his people. However, many individuals I've encountered on my journey have been there for seasons and not the entirety. Some people I've had to break away from and some people God simply removed from my life. This is all part of the journey. Either way, we should invest in people on our journey and ask God to help us navigate these relationships.

Be Obedient

Success along this journey will depend on our level of

obedience and humility. If we want to run the race of salvation with patience and cross the finishing line strong, then we will have to be obedient to God and walk humbly before him. Many chosen ones that have gone before us started their journey on the right path. However, Satan has managed to cause them to fall just before they reach the finishing line. Their paths have diverted away from God, and instead they've chased after fame, notoriety, mammon, and filthy lucre. God cannot use a corrupted vessel. It is through humility and obedience that we transform into vessels of honour.

On this journey, God has had to push me to the forefront. In general, I do not like attention or the spotlight – it makes me feel uncomfortable. However, the Lord has placed on me a spirit of boldness when necessary, and when I speak up, people tend to pay attention and listen. I just obey God and do what he tells me to do. It's as simple as that. For some reason, this has caused some people in and outside of the body of Christ to become irritated. On observation of these people, I note that they can't seem to understand why or how I move so differently. At first look, I appear quiet and low key – very unassuming. But when I use my voice or my gifts or talents, they seem to get angry – some of them didn't expect certain things from me. My modus operandi has always been to obey God despite detractors and naysayers.

Be steadfast and obedient. God will make space for you where he wills, even at the expense of other people's pride. Also, be humble and patient when dealing with people on the journey. Like David, we will even have to obey and humble ourselves before corrupt people such as Saul. Our meekness and obedience will show forth the fruits of the Spirit and cause us to have an effective witness.

Get Back Up

Us chosen people are good at making mistakes. Just look at Samson, Moses, David, Aaron, Jonah, Peter, and others. Because we are human, we will make mistakes and fall short. Where God gets the glory is when we get back up! One day as I was communing with God in prayer, Holy Spirit said, *"You'll make mistakes along the way Cam, but come to me and I will help."* God wants to be our Helper when we fall. The Word says that a righteous man falls seven times, but he gets back up (Proverbs 24:16)! Staying in the ring and completing the mission of fighting the good fight requires the "get back up" spirit. A defeated soul doesn't stand a chance gaining the victory. So, keep going – *push*. Tell God where you fell short – he understands. He'll strengthen your legs after each fall so that your muscles gain more capacity for the good work of the Kingdom. I've made many mistakes. Said things I shouldn't have. Did things I shouldn't have. But the one thing that keeps me going is God telling me, *"I'm so proud of you and I'm pleased with you."* So, I get back up, knowing that the journey is completed well through diligence and resilience.

PRAYER WALK CONVERSATION

I had gone on a weekend vacation with a friend during summer. The Airbnb we stayed in was beautifully laid out surrounded by a gorgeous pond, walking paths, bridges, gardens, and sunlight that had the right hues and cast a pretty glow of pink, purple, and orange. It was late evening, and after a tiring day, I decided to take a walk. The decision came because I was in a very brooding mood, upset at some earlier events, and I wanted to take some space to get fresh air and stretch my legs. As I made my way outside to the front of the house, I took a left and started walking on the sidewalk until I reached the path that meandered along the pond.

I started talking to Holy Spirit as I walked, and he started talking back to me. I began venting about various things. Stuff I needed to get off my chest; I unloaded to him at record pace. God was used to my style of venting, so he listened until I got everything out. But instead of addressing some of the things I brought up, he changed subjects and started speaking to me about my future. Now it was my turn to listen to him. The Lord started talking to me about my unique personality, calling, and the things he would be using me to do for him in the coming years. He began to describe some of the plans he wanted me to execute, and how he was proud of how far I had come. By the time I made the loop around the spectacular scenery of the area and returned to the Airbnb, I was refreshed, calm, and expectant of the blessings of God.

What I had experienced was a journey. A walk with just God and I communicating with each other. My vacation prayer walk was exactly what God wants to do with us on our journey. He wants to hear our opinions and thoughts, but he also wants to relay his agenda so we can live it out. At the end of the journey, we become refreshed, at peace, and in expectant awe of our reward of eternal life. The walk took patience, and slowing down occasionally to notice the ducks, the dog walkers, the sounds of water, the beautiful flowers, and everything in between. Likewise, our journey will require patience and slowing down to thank and appreciate God for everything he is doing for us along the way, even despite challenges and obstacles. It is relationship with Christ as a chosen one that allows us to walk the journey with confidence.

I must say that looking back, one major thing that has kept me walking the journey out has been the fear of the Lord. It was the fear of the Lord that kept me from perversion. It was the fear of the Lord that has caused me to avoid giving into anger. The fear of the Lord taught me to walk humbly and circumspectly, and in turn God gave me grace to combat everything the enemy has thrown at me. Through every hard thing and uncomfortable moment, the fear of the Lord and the relationship I have with him has given me momentum to keep pursuing God and my calling.

My whole journey so far, I've always thought myself to be an outlier, and truly, I have been just that. I viewed myself being different as a negative thing, but God had to change my thinking. I'm not crazy, weird, or a misfit at all. I am chosen, called, set apart, and destined for greatness. May I always see myself as God's chosen, walking each day moment by moment with Master Jesus.

The chosen journey is a life where a death is daily lived and at the end, the chosen arise alive in Christ forevermore. Amen.

....

"I press toward the mark for the prize of the high calling of God in Christ Jesus."

Philippians 3:14

15 | PRAYERS FOR THE CHOSEN

"Continue in prayer, and watch in the same with thanksgiving."
Colossians 4:2

Since this book is all about sharing, I decided to share some of the prayers that I continue to pray along the journey. Prayer is such an important aspect of a chosen one's walk. Not only does prayer keep us connected to the Heavenly Father, but it also has power to break yokes, destroy the plans of the enemy, and usher in the will of God according to his Word. You can pray these on your own chosen journey.

CHOSEN PRAYER

Father, thank you for choosing and anointing me for the high calling of God. I boldly speak your reviving Word over my life and destiny and declare that I am chosen for such a time as this, to know and worship you in spirit and in truth, while being strengthened by your power and the Holy Spirit to perform exploits, in Jesus' name. I declare that I am your battle axe, and a vessel of honour fit for the Master's use. I confess that I will use my tongue as a weapon to call forth those things that be not as

though they were, as I activate my faith in you and your Word. I command my God-given destiny to come into alignment with the will of the Father, in Jesus' name. I put on the full armour of God and cover myself, my family, my properties, and my assets with the blood of Jesus. I cancel by the blood of Jesus every plot, plan, scheme, and ploy of the enemy to oppress, kill, steal, and destroy my life and purpose. I withdraw by fire my spiritual virtues and inheritances from the cages of the enemy, in Jesus' name. Lord, fill me with the knowledge of your will in all spiritual wisdom and understanding. Lead me by your Holy Spirit into all truth and order my steps in your Word. In Jesus' mighty name.
Amen.

A PRAYER FOR DISCERNMENT & REVELATION

Heavenly Father,

Give me the spirit of wisdom and revelation in the knowledge of you. I pray that the eyes of my heart (the very center and core of my being) may be enlightened (and flooded with light by the Holy Spirit), so that I will know, understand, and discern the spiritual realm around me, the physical world I live in, the will of the LORD, and the plans of the enemy, in Jesus' name. Lord, grant me eyes to see, ears to hear, and a heart that understands spiritually and accurately, in Jesus' name. Open my eyes that I may see and know the secrets of God and the mysteries of the Spirit. Anoint my spiritual eyes, ears, and heart for the good work of the Kingdom of God, in Jesus' name.
Amen.

FIRE PRAYERS

<u>Note</u>: The "enemy" or "enemies" I speak of in the following prayers are in reference to demonic spiritual entities or forces and **not** human beings. We are to bless those that curse us and forgive those who wrong us. God will not honour prayers where humans created in his image are cursed. Also, these prayers should be used once you put on the full armour of God (Ephesians 6) and cover yourself and your loved ones with the blood of Jesus.

1. I loose the Lord's bed of suffering upon Jezebels operating against me, in Jesus' name (Rev. 2:20-22).

2. My Father, let the enemy's table become a snare to them, in Jesus' name (Ps. 69:22).

3. In the name of Jesus, I command the eyes of monitoring spirits watching me to be darkened (Ps. 69:23).

4. In the name of Jesus, I loose myself from the cords of the wicked (Ps. 129:4).

5. I short-circuit every demonic device used to target and attack my life and blessings, in Jesus' name.

6. Let the fear of the wicked incensed against me come upon him, in Jesus' name.

7. I command the release of the north wind to blow supernatural provision and increase over my life, in Jesus' name.

8. Father, give me wisdom that causes me to inherit substance and treasures, in Jesus' name (Prov. 8:21).

9. I bind and release the fire of judgement on spirits of

confusion, lust, perversion, depression, fear, lack, death, sickness, poverty, delay, and witchcraft attacking me, in Jesus' name.

10. Let the shrines of the wicked be impotent, in the name of Jesus.

11. I destroy the cauldrons, pots, calabashes, and crystal balls of witches cursing me with the fire of God, in Jesus' name.

12. I use the dynamite of heaven to destroy evil altars prophesying against me, in Jesus' name.

13. I de-program every form of wickedness and evil that the enemy has planted against me in the sun, moon, stars, earth, and waters with the blood of Jesus, in Jesus' name.

14. Let everlasting confusion cleave to the camp of my enemies, in Jesus' name.

15. I release the drought of the Lord against marine spirits targeting me, in the name of Jesus.

16. I loose the hook of the Lord to destroy marine and serpentine spirits afflicting me, in Jesus' name.

17. My Father, send the angel of the Lord to war against principalities fighting against me, in Jesus' name.

18. Let the blessing that maketh rich and adds no sorrow be appointed and released to me today, in Jesus' name.

19. My Father, be a terror unto them that seek to trouble me, in Jesus' name.

20. My Father, release your angelic hunters to set traps for my enemies, in Jesus' name.

21. Let thorns and thistles be the portion of them cursing my life, ministry, family, and business, in Jesus' name.

22. My Father, release your angelic assassins to remove the enemy warring against my destiny, in Jesus' name.

23. I bind familiar spirits associated with my bloodline to the bones of my ancestors who worshipped them, in Jesus' name.

24. In the name of Jesus, I sever the silver cord of witches and warlocks astral projecting into my environment or my dreams. Father, let them be trapped forever, in Jesus' name.

25. I loose the sun to smite my enemies by day, in the name of Jesus.

26. I loose the moon to smite the enemy of my destiny by night, in Jesus' name.

27. I loose confusion and civil war into the camp of my enemies today, in Jesus' name.

28. I cancel the cry of evil blood sacrifices offered up to curse my life by the blood of Jesus, in Jesus' name.

29. I loose the terrible tempest of the Lord to uproot the plans of the enemy concerning my family, in the name of Jesus.

30. I loose the Lord's arrows of judgement and death against the strongman warring against my soul, in Jesus' name.

31. By the blood of Jesus, I cancel and break every curse, spell, hex, vex, jinx, enchantment, incantation, and evil invocation issued against my life, family, ministry, business, property, and finances, in Jesus' name.

32. I overrule demonic objections concerning my life, marriage, business, and ministry through the blood of Jesus, in Jesus' name.

33. In the name of Jesus, I bind the terror by night and the enemy's arrows by day.

34. Lord, release your reaping angels to assist me with ministering the Gospel of Jesus Christ to others, in the name of Jesus.

35. I abort the plans of the enemy to destroy my purpose with the sword of the Lord, in the name of Jesus.

36. I command wicked conceptions against my success, elevation, and prosperity to miscarry by the fire of God, in Jesus' name.

37. In the name and by the blood of Jesus, I command every virus, bacteria, parasite, and harmful toxin to die immediately upon contact with my body. I legislate by the authority to decree a thing according to Job 22:28, that you shall not harm me and impact my health, in Jesus' name. I command my bones, organs, tissues, and cells to come into divine alignment and optimal functioning, in Jesus' name.

38. Blood of Jesus, fight for me today!

After praying the above prayers, you can pray this sealing prayer below:

SEALING PRAYER

In the name of Jesus, I bind all spirits of backlash and retaliation due to praying these prayers and cancel their plans by the power God has given me to trample upon serpents and scorpions. I declare no weapon formed against me shall prosper and nothing by any means shall harm me or my family and those things which pertain to us, in the name of Jesus. I seal these prayers with the blood of Jesus, and Lord, I thank you for hearing me and answering according to your will. Amen.

BIBLICAL AFFIRMATIONS

1. I declare that I am fruitful, and I multiply abundantly, in Jesus' name.

2. I perform signs, wonders, and miracles by the power of the Holy Ghost.

3. My seed and bloodline will be set apart for Yahweh's use.

4. I prophesy the word of God with accuracy and power, in Jesus' name.

5. I am a carrier of God's glory and anointing.

6. I shall flourish like a palm tree and grow like a cedar in Lebanon.

7. I shall be recompensed in the earth more than the wicked and the sinner.

8. I live under an open heaven.

9. I shall lend and not borrow.

10. My territory is expanding and my borders extending. I increase in divine capacity in the spirit.

11. My blessings shall not be aborted or miscarried.

12. I am a creative vessel in the hand of the Lord.

13. I am blessed with spiritual blessings in heavenly places.

14. Angels encamp around me, my family, and my home.

15. I receive the oil of joy on my life.

16. I invite the presence of the Holy Spirit in my life, home, ministry, workplace, and business.

17. I shall not die but live to declare God's works.

18. The afflictions and diseases of Egypt shall not cleave to me, for I follow the commands of the Lord.

19. I trust in God's timing, provision, and instructions.

20. I lack no good thing, and I am preserved by God's hand.

21. I receive the peace of God that guards my heart and mind in Christ Jesus.

22. I receive dunamis, exousia, and kratos power from the Holy Ghost.

23. I am empowered by the Holy Spirit to empower and transform the lives of others.

24. I receive faith that comes from hearing the word of God.

25. The Lord's favour surrounds me as a shield. I live abundantly.

26. The Lord is my Strong Tower. In him I have safety, comfort, life, and prosperity.

27. I give cheerfully and generously to the poor and needy and to ministry as acts of worship. I will reap the blessings and favour of the Lord.

28. I shall have favour with God and man. I operate in the earth as a privileged child of the King. Exceptions and

exemptions in courts, councils, business arenas, financial institutions, political realms, and spheres of influence are legislated by heaven on my behalf in alignment with God's will.

29. I am a mover and shaker in the earth for the Kingdom of God. Wherever I go, I will influence people to live for Jesus Christ.

30. I will prosper and be in good health even as my soul prospers.

31. The wealth of the wicked is transferred into my hand.

32. I receive supernatural grace to walk on the chosen journey with Christ Jesus.

33. My ministry shall be a haven to heal the broken and weary. Revival fire is breaking out over my area of jurisdiction.

34. I am more than a conqueror in Christ Jesus. I rise with humility above setbacks and opposition. Hell is vanquished by the power of Jesus, therefore, every evil coming against me is defeated and cursed.

35. I am of the violent generation in the Kingdom of God who take my possessions and inheritances by force.

36. I am a vessel of honour and fit for the Master's use. My life will be one lived well and a testimony of the greatness of Jehovah.

16 | QUESTIONS FOR THE CHOSEN

"If any of you lack wisdom, let him ask of God, that giveth to all men liberally, and upbraideth not; and it shall be given him."
James 1:5

If you know that you are a chosen one and still have questions or uncertainties about your path and what God wants you to do, then you are not alone. This is the time and season to inquire of the Lord about your journey, and what he wants and expects specifically from you. It will help you to know the next steps you should take.

Below are some questions I've had to ask and pray about myself. If you know the answers to some or all of the questions, then congratulations! You've got a great start, just keep going. If you don't know, however, ask these questions and get the answers you need. Pray about them and find out what God's vision for your life looks like.

1.) When was your first life-changing encounter with God?

QUESTIONS

2.) What has God revealed to you that needs addressing in your foundation?

3.) What do you want your legacy as a chosen one to be?

4.) How does God like to communicate with you? What vision for your life has he downloaded to you?

5.) What will your ministry for Jesus look like?

6.) What is your calling in Christ Jesus?

7.) In what location does God want you to build in his Kingdom?

QUESTIONS

8.) What are the gifts and talents God has given to you, and how does he want you to use them?

9.) What do you want your impact for Jesus to look like on your generation?

10.) What are you currently willing to change about yourself and your life for the glory of God?

11.) Who in the Bible had a similar calling to yours? How did they navigate their chosen journey?

12.) What personal strategies has God given to you to evolve in spiritual warfare and advancement?

If you have any questions about this book or would like to offer feedback, scan the QR code below (or visit the contact page at our website: https://www.chayilworkspublishing.com) and let us know what you think:

To follow-up with future projects by this author, please visit:
www.chayilworkspublishing.com

YOU ARE CHOSEN

A Product of Love

A Person of Destiny

A Bearer of Fruit

A Teller of Truth

A Set Apart Gift

Chosen, for such a time as this

ABOUT THE AUTHOR

Camille Springer is a Bajan-Canadian author of works inspired by the Holy Spirit. With a BSc. in Forensic Science and over 5 years of social services experience, she's on a mission to share the Gospel of Jesus Christ and further build in the Kingdom of God. She's currently studying broadcasting and recently launched a business in pursuit of becoming a media practitioner. In her spare time, she enjoys researching, writing, reading, making music, and serving at her church.

You can connect with Camille at chayilworkspub@gmail.com.

www.ingramcontent.com/pod-product-compliance
Lightning Source LLC
Chambersburg PA
CBHW022056160426
43198CB00008B/250